To

_____

From

_____

Recommendations

"It takes tremendous inner growth, combined with deep study of the human journey of transformation, to reach the insights that Kawtar shares in this book. Each one is powerful and is up there with some of the finest work I have read on leadership and personal evolution. Unabashedly so! What a gift to leaders and people everywhere. This book is all about integrating the elements of heart, mind, and soul, and gloriously and authentically stepping into your own story.

Urja Shah
President of Setco Foundation,
CSR Director for the Setco Group of companies, India

"'I' has reached its limit. Without abandoning 'I,' our human family now needs to develop the fullness of 'We'—Conscious Togetherness. 'We' is the way forward. We need 'We' to solve our collective problems and take humanity to its next evolutionary level. This book is a beacon helping light this new path. Buy it, read it, and watch how it contributes to your 'We' and to a much better world."

Martin Rutte
Founder, www.ProjectHeavenOnEarth.com

"What is modern life asking from us? How do we lead ourselves, and how do we interact with others? These questions are not always common to ask ourselves.

Since the first moment I met Kawtar a few years ago, I was struck by her authenticity, her powerful and carefully chosen communication, and her truly extraordinary, developed skill of deep listening. In my life, she is a person on my list of 'who to contact to discover blind spots whether that is a thought, a feeling, or a physical symptom.' I trust her because she will be there for me without any judgments and always get to the point. Now that her book is here, the whole world can have access to Kawtar's wisdom!

This book is a guide for all of us readers who are willing to take the steps to a purposeful life without any vagueness. Her story, solid background information, honest shares, and practical examples and exercises help us to integrate all the steps ourselves. Kawtar invites us, and challenges us, to take the necessary steps to break through the limiting patterns that keep us from living a fulfilled, purposeful, aligned life.

This isn't just another self-development book because it is written by Kawtar, who is living proof, walking the talk that we all can become conscious leaders, starting with leading ourselves and from there be the change the world needs now more than ever."

Nienke van Bezooijen
TEDx Speaker Coach

"Kawtar brings to this book simplicity and authenticity that speaks to the heart and taps into our essence—our collective potential as human beings. In her work, there lies the hope for understanding what we must arrest, and hence change, about how we function and think and validate within us. This book inspires us to look at new ways of being and doing. It is a call to revealing the true essence of what it means to be humans who cocreate on this planet."

Vikram Bhatt
Founder, Leadership That Works India

"Kawtar's insight is shining a light and creating a path for anyone who wants a deeper understanding of what it means to be human.

Unfolding Peace is a book to do inner work that is not always easy to do and will begin to open up the Being you were born to be by aligning your power through vulnerability, while honoring and healing your spirit to awaken and connect to the people we truly are. This book is a gift and much more. It is filled with practical inner work to have us discover the journey that will leave a positive impact for what our soul is calling for with love and peace."

Wendy Schneider

"This book is a must-read for everyone brave enough to take a long journey to their closest and farthest point of self. The reader knows that it is a hard and a long journey but also acknowledges that the end of the journey is a rewarding one, and patience is a good friend. It was an enlightening experience to read this brilliant book and have Kawtar's company during our inner self-journey, which gave us the support and the encouragement to choose the light. It was also a pleasure being a part of this book as well and I hope everyone enjoys it as much as I did!"

Birsu Karaarslan, MA Development Studies
Former President of the Feminist Collective
and the Gender, Peace and Security Coalition

"This piece of art that Kawtar has written is not just a book — it's a life-changing 'deep conversation' that shakes you out of everything and anything that has been bogging you down. I really appreciate how the book does not just stop at abstract talk and quotes. Instead, it delves into the science and practical methods by which you can change your life RIGHT HERE, RIGHT NOW. Above all, I appreciate Kawtar's willingness to open up about her personal experience of struggle; her vulnerability made me feel validated and gave me the courage to begin taking care of my own emotional state. Especially at a time in which everyone all around the world feels so stuck and helpless, I hope this book can be a beacon of hope, and the start of something amazing within each and every person."

Jiwon Lee
Author, *The Third Culture Teen*

Unfolding Peace

9 Leadership Principles to Create Cultures of Well-being, Belonging, and Peace

by

Kawtar El Alaoui

Copyright © 2022 *by Kawtar El Alaoui*

All rights reserved. No part of this book may be reproduced or transmitted in any form or by any means, electronic or mechanical, including photocopying, recording, or by an information storage and retrieval system without written permission of the publisher, except for the inclusions of brief quotations in review.

Disclaimer: The Publisher and the Author does not guarantee that anyone following the techniques, suggestions, tips, ideas, or strategies will become successful. The advice and strategies contained herein may not be suitable for every situation. The Publisher and Author shall have neither liability nor responsibility to anyone with respect to any loss or damage caused, or alleged to be caused, directly or indirectly by the information in this book.

Any citations or a potential source of information from other organizations or websites given herein does not mean that the Author or Publisher endorses the information/content the website or organization provides or recommendations it may make. It is the readers' responsibility to do their own due diligence when researching information. Also, websites listed or referenced herein may have changed or disappeared from the time that this work was created and the time that it is read.

Saved By Story Publishing, LLC
Prescott, AZ
www.SavedByStory.house

Unfolding Peace (1st edition)

Paperback: 978-0-9887809-8-9
eBook: 978-0-9887809-9-6

Cover by Alyssa Noelle Coelho and Lionheart Creations
Interior Design by Dawn Teagarden
Photo by Abraham Aristide

Acknowledgments

To the benevolent force that has carried me through the darkest times—the co-creative force we call consciousness—that creates shifts in the physical world every time I do my inner work, thank you.

To My Family, By Blood or Soul Connection

To my daughter Suzy, for being the catalyst of my journey. My life changed forever the day I realized I was accepting things for myself I would not have accepted for you. I love you.

To my husband Jonathon, for believing in me and being my sounding board, my friend, and my partner in this crazy adventure called life. Thank you for holding down the home front with love and support, so that I could take the time and space needed to not only heal but thrive in my new career.

To my parents, I am grateful to you for bringing me to life and laying a firm foundation for my soul lessons. Despite difficult times, I believe we were each doing our best with the limited knowledge, tools, and worldview we had. To my grandfather, Yazid, your presence in my childhood planted more seeds for this book than I can articulate. Thank you for your love and feeling of safety.

To my mom, Achira, thank you for being a constant pillar of strength. To my brothers, Anas, Yassine, and Taha, I am grateful for each of you. In my eyes, you have been more than just brothers. You have each been co-travelers in reversing the unhealthy generational patterns we inherited. To Anas, for having been there since the beginning, and for the difficult experiences we moved through together, I am grateful for your wisdom and kindness. I love each of you, and whichever one of you is with me at the time is my favorite brother. :-)

To my first mother-in-law, Hoda, you were an angel in the most dire and critical circumstances. Your kindness, courage, integrity, and independence inspire me. To my stepmom, Karima, and my current in-laws, Kathy and Victor, you have each been a source of strength, love, and growth. I am so grateful for your loving presence.

To Ashraf, words fail to express my gratitude for your professionalism and your compassionate heart while you were ensuring my and my daughter's return to safety.

To my dear friends and cousin, Sarah, Nadia, and Ananta, you have been steady sources of strength, growth, kindness, care, and inspiration. I love you and I am so grateful to have you in my life.

To All of My Past and Present Mentors, Coaches, and Healers

To Danielle Turcotte, you nurtured my inquisitive and ambitious spirit in law school and planted the seeds of confidence that enabled me to leave an abusive marriage against all odds. I am forever grateful to have been your student and mentee.

To my closest mentors and colleagues (in the order you came into my life): Kareen Aristide, Isabelle Min, Vikram Bhatt, Guthrie Sayen, Dr. Niki Elliott, Martin Rutte, Martha Lasley, Nienke van Bezooijen, Sandra Epstein, Wendy Schneider, and Dr. Scilla Elworthy. My journey has been immensely enriched by the diversity of your paths and your wisdom, kindness, and humility.

To the many coaches, therapists, healers, and peers who have supported my journey. They say it takes a village. It is certainly true for healing. My heart is deeply grateful for each of you, the healing power of your presence, and the empowering tools you each share with the world.

To Nancy Coco, thank you for being a container for the early ramblings that gave birth to this book. It took years of pre-writing as you predicted. I am grateful for your care, empathy, and kindness.

To Nikita Sura Sheth, who was instrumental in bringing this book to life. Your support and mentorship as a writing coach were invaluable.[1]

To Amanda Johnson, you have held the container for this book to come to life with a rare combination of professionalism, integrity, and alignment. I am grateful to you and for all you have become to midwife these life-changing books.

To My Clients

Each of you has allowed me to learn and grow with you along your journeys. I admire you for your resilience, courage, and determination to build better lives for yourselves and a better world for everyone whose lives you touch. Thank you for co-creating the spaces that allowed me to see these principles in action. Our work has contributed to much more than just us.

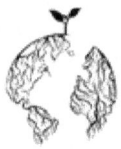

To My Community

To the Conscious Togetherness clients, team members, and past, present, and future allies—there are no words to express my gratitude. For the first half of my life, I felt "out of place" and longed for the type of safety, transparency, self-responsibility, and purpose-sharing that we are experiencing in this community.

Thank you for being such amazing allies!

To the many inner work communities of practice I am a part of, your support has been invaluable in creating environments of deep exploration, self-knowledge, accountability, and growth at all levels. Thank you.

To all of the readers who previewed this book, thank you for your time and your feedback. This book is more powerful because of you. A special thank you to Isla and Gert from the Mighty Heart Community for your thorough feedback.

To allies and challengers who do not see their name yet know they have been an important part of my journey, thank you for your role in my life.

To the Lands I Have Lived On

To Morocco, the land that I was born in. Thank you for all I received in my early years. I am particularly proud and grateful to have graduated from a public high school. I hold immense gratitude for my teachers, especially those who taught economics and Islamic studies. I hope to give back more than I received.

To Egypt, for the valuable life lessons, the most beautiful diving experiences, and the wonderful, kind, and honest people who reached in and showed me that all perspectives exist everywhere and that no country, religion, culture, or people can be reduced to their stereotypes.

To South Korea and India, for enriching my human experience with valuable lessons, ancient wisdom, deep insights, and unforgettable memories.

To Canada, the land I learned to call home as a teenager and young adult. Even as I grappled to find a sense of belonging after traumatic events, resources and support were always available.

I am grateful to the Faculté de Droit, Université de Montréal, especially Liette Malouin, and Sophie Arès for the support I received as a single mother in my last year of law school.

I am grateful to the welfare, health care, and education systems in Québec and Ontario that enabled me to reconstruct a life after leaving everything behind.

I am grateful to the Canadian Center for Addiction and Mental Health (CAMH) at the University of Toronto where my mother worked for years. You have helped bring the mental health conversation into my life and begin to remove shame around it.

I am grateful to TV Ontario where my mom worked for many years.

I am grateful to the Taggart Family Y daycare services in Ottawa for the support I received as a single mom that enabled me to finish my legal studies, especially to Sylvie Madely who has been a family friend, a role model, and a loving presence in my life.

To the foreign service officers who work tirelessly for Canadians abroad, I have seen firsthand the difference you make, and I am grateful for your support in time of need.

I respectfully acknowledge that this book has been written on the unceded Territory of the Anishinaabe Algonquin Nation.

Canada, while we have much healing to do as a nation, we have much to be proud of and build upon.

May we all find our way to wholeness and peace,

Kawtar

Contents

Foreword 19

Dear Reader 21

Introduction
Surrendering to the Unfolding 23

Chapter 1
The Arrogance of Intellect 51

Chapter 2
The Power of Vulnerability 69

Chapter 3
The Freedom of Choice 87

Chapter 4
The Reclamation of Inner Power 109

Chapter 5
The Empowerment of Meeting Needs 129

Chapter 6
The Holism of Self-Care 145

Chapter 7
The Inevitability of Interdependence 165

Chapter 8
The Relief of Self-Leadership 197

Chapter 9
The Realization of Peace and Purpose 218

Conclusion
From Inner Work to Leadership Outcomes 239

A Special Invitation 244

About Kawtar.. 245

Endnotes 247

Foreword

by Dr. Scilla Elworthy

Founder, Business Plan for Peace
3-time Nominee for the Nobel Peace Prize

Peacebuilding has been my passion and calling from an early age. When I was thirteen years old, I watched on an old TV as Soviet tanks pounded into Budapest in 1956, killing teenagers like me. I stormed upstairs to pack my bags to help out. My mother came up and asked what I was doing. When I told her, she said, "Scilla, you are too young to help now; but if you will just unpack your bags, I'll see that you get trained." And she did.

As soon as I could, I worked in refugee camps and with people risking their lives so that others don't get killed. I also worked with leaders to build ways of getting rid of nuclear weapons and founded Peace Direct to support locally-led peace building. Over five decades, what I've learned is that the education we need is not only of the mind but of the *heart*. To bring about real change in the world requires that we develop our Inner Power. I share how this can be done in my books, including *Pioneering the Possible, The Business Plan for Peace,* and *The Mighty Heart.*

I got to know Kawtar during my online course for *The Mighty Heart*. I greatly admire the process of looking inward that has enabled Kawtar to write the book you have in your hands now. Her honesty in assessing her own experience will be helpful to all readers who are beginning the vital journey of self-knowledge—an essential one for people who wish to activate their courage and implement solutions to humanity's complex challenges, in integrated ways. She uses solid and structured research, practical examples, and exercises to integrate what she shares. We need people like Kawtar, who walk the talk, listen deeply, and support others to lead by example.

Dear Reader

As you read this book, especially the parts in which I have shared my story, you might notice big feelings rising to the surface.

I have attempted to share enough of my personal experience to give you insights into the journeys that enabled my learnings, but not so much that you feel overwhelmed by the details and emotions that may be strangely close to your own.

In all my years of coaching and supporting others, I have discovered that many of the traumas I have suffered, and the dynamics that led to and perpetuated them, are not unique to me. They are, in fact, all too common.

And, if we are to create a better, more peaceful world, we must bring them into the light, process the pain, and find pathways forward together.

Despite my efforts to find the balance of sharing without triggering, you may still find yourself feeling strong emotions in the places where you carry similar wounds or unresolved narratives. If that happens, I encourage you to allow yourself the time and space needed to heal.

I invite you to read mindfully, at your own pace, and pause for self-care and reflection if you find yourself triggered. If necessary, speak with a professional.

While these insights came through crisis and traumatic experiences, I have learned to appreciate the vital importance of living from inquiry, presence, and for higher possibilities—for individuals and the larger collective. That is the leadership journey I invite you into through this book: Leadership for a better you, and a better world, from the inside-out.

INTRODUCTION

Surrendering to the Unfolding

"If I can't make this work, my life will be over. I don't know how to do anything other than being a lawyer…" I could barely get the words out between tears that wouldn't stop while my boyfriend did his best to reassure me over the phone. Ten minutes earlier, suddenly gripped by an intense moment of panic, I'd run out of the building, unable to make sense of what I was feeling. Hysterical tears took over as I realized what had prompted it. Hearing yet another colleague share how they had been treated by the senior manager had triggered me beyond what I could stomach.

How are bullies in leadership positions? How can this exist in Canada? Any day now, my security clearance will come through, and I will finally get my position at the Department of Justice (DOJ). Why is it taking so long? What about my life could possibly justify this treatment again? How long will I have to pay for being muslim? Haven't I paid enough already?

For a moment, I forgot my boyfriend was on the phone while I sat at the edge of the planter on the street walk, crying frantically.

Finally, he said, "Do you need me to take the afternoon off and come pick you up and take you home? I don't think you should drive yourself home today."

I am a single mom. I have to keep it together and be brave through this no matter what. My daughter and I need my income. I felt so ashamed of myself, crying, feeling like I had lost all control over my emotions. Looking around at the few pedestrians and their sideways glances, I wanted the earth to open up and swallow me; but I knew how to suck it up and move on. I have to keep it together. *Failure is not an option. I have been to hell and back. I cannot let this stop me. I have to get back to the office and be professional.*

Finally, I stopped crying. "Thank you. I'll be okay. I'm going to finish my day…" I said goodbye, fixed my jacket, and walked back into the building. After washing my face in the bathroom, I returned to my desk, quietly praying for an uneventful afternoon. The best we hoped for some days was that the boss would leave everyone alone. How she went around destroying everyone's spirit in total impunity was beyond me.

If I can just keep my head down long enough, I will be out of this place.

But the downward spiral happened faster than I could have anticipated. From that moment on, my health deteriorated, with every passing day, with every interaction with her. She was the only person I had confided in when the other bully had attacked me, and I could never have guessed how toxic she was herself at the time. In fact, the day I had that meltdown, I did not realize she was targeting me, too. Family and friends were seeing warning signs and advising me to leave for another department; but without my clearance, it was hard to move around.

How is it that I keep finding myself dealing with such toxic, abusive people? What is wrong with me? I just want peace. Why do I keep finding myself stuck in toxicity and abuse?

This was the beginning of my journey of healing, which took me back to the origin of this dynamic in my life.

"If you make my brother sleep outside, I will leave with him." This is one of my earliest memories. At five years of age, I felt I had to stand between my brother and father to stop my father's aggression. A few months earlier, I had witnessed my father chase my mother out of our home, in a very public outburst. The fear of that moment steeped deep into my bones and planted a seed. Now, just a few months later, with my mother gone and my father unable to control his emotions, I had to be the adult in the room.

I had to be the peacemaker.

At only five years old, while I wouldn't have been able to articulate what I was doing or why, I was negotiating peace deals between a rebellious brother and an angry father. What made it even more difficult was that my father's outbursts were not frequent or directed toward everyone. But, occasionally, he would go into this altered state and become a different person, so it was hard to see him as the bad guy. I felt very unsafe when this side of him would get triggered; and though I did not realize it at the time, the fear remained ever-present below the surface. To feel safe, I had to erase my own fear, make excuses for my dad's behavior, and try to soothe his temper. I had to do anything to keep the peace, including suppressing my distress and pain.

This was inside the house. As soon as I stepped out, it was a different story. Publicly, my father looked like a loving, kind, and caring father who took on the role of single parenting his kids after a bitter divorce. He looked like the hero. He was a highly-educated man. A rising star in his career. Climbing the ranks of status, and with an influential family name, he was both respected and feared.

I grew up in a beautiful gated community in Casablanca, Morocco, a leader in my own right in my group of about twenty friends. After school, we'd do homework at someone's house and enjoy delicious Moroccan mint tea, with cookies, or homemade sandwiches, accompanied by olives and olive oil on the side. After snack time, we'd go out to play soccer or tennis, climb trees, or ride our bikes to the market to get bread for dinner, all the while making no distinction between boys and girls. That is, until the age of ten. Suddenly, my father began to censor the clothes I wore, the way I spoke, and how I spent my time.

Short skirts were not okay. Hanging out with boys was no longer appropriate. I was not allowed to be out after sunset, as it was deemed inappropriate and unrespectable for a girl from a "good family" to be hanging out after dark.

Speaking my mind in my usual directness became a big *no-no*. So, I learned to hold my thoughts in, as much as was

Surrendering to the Unfolding

humanly possible; but even then, my basic nature appeared to be too much, even when I censored myself.

At the time, these restrictions didn't feel linked to religion as much as to our culture. Everyone around me seemed to agree that Islam was about the essence, being a good person and neighbour, and living the five pillars to the best of our ability. Many would say an important tenet of Islam was to never judge anyone or assume their relationship with God; only God had that privilege.

I remember seeing French nuns, walking in their black habits on their way to the market and thinking nothing of it. I remember friends from Spain, neighbors from France, friends attending Jewish schools, and others who went to French schools. Being different did not carry a negative connotation as it seems to in the West. In fact, I learned to love diversity in Morocco.

In school, we learned how Islam had empowered women and their position in society. They kept their family name upon marriage, ran businesses, and kept their earnings from work when Islam was established as a religion. We also learned that the man's role was to be responsible and provide and care for women and the family.

Culture, on the other hand, had these rigid gender roles and stereotypes. As a girl, I was treated very differently than my brother. When I experienced harm, it was assumed that I had done something wrong, which compounded my pain. There was the time the maid hit me and was allowed to continue working for us as if it had never happened. Then, the time a neighbor assaulted me, and I was further hurt at home because it was deemed my fault without so much as a question about what actually happened.

To keep the peace, I had to not only suppress my distress and needs, but also allow others to hurt me, keep quiet about it, and even pay the price for their assaults on me. What I had to say was irrelevant. The harm I had experienced was inconsequential. Only perceptions mattered. Being a good girl meant smiling while being assaulted, keeping quiet while being abused, and catering to egos, even when devastated. This is how suppression, appeasement, and dissociation became ingrained survival mechanisms. It was the price for "peace," "safety," and "belonging."

And this is the dynamic that plagued my life and replicated in relationships and workplaces.

My freedom as a teenager was limited to going to the club where we would have access to the swimming pools, tennis courts, restaurants, and other activities. Outside those walls, however, my outings were confined to attending school.

During summers in Canada with my mom and her new husband, I witnessed quite the contrast. Watching teenage girls dress any way they wished, hanging out with friends, even bringing boyfriends to their family gatherings was mind-boggling. I felt envious of their ability to work and earn at such a young age. I loved the openness they had, the freedom, and the trust to make decisions for their own lives.

Meanwhile, during school years back in Morocco, I felt enormous pressure to be perfect. Between my father's rigid rules for my life and his status, my behavior had to be irreproachable by cultural standards. And with my father's temper ever-present behind his deceiving smile, I gave up having a teenage life.

The clear message was this: A young woman's entire worth is tied to her reputation. It is like currency. Having relationships with boys would ruin my reputation, virtually making me "unmarriable." I had to be very selective about my friends to ensure my parents approved of them. I always felt stuck between the two worlds. Neither fully Moroccan nor fully Canadian.

To keep the peace at home, and avoid anything that could be deemed shameful, I had turned my attention to my beloved studies and focused my time and efforts on my younger brothers. This was also a great way to keep the peace with my step-mom, too. In our culture at the time, once a man remarried, it was a given that the new family would live riddled with conflict. Outsiders never thought twice when they counseled me to rebel against my step-mom, but I didn't see the sense in giving my dad ultimatums when he had chosen her and had children with her.

Determined to not poison the well, I suppressed my own needs and pain. I channeled my energy toward befriending my step-mom and making peace at home, while I focused on navigating the path to becoming a lawyer. Of course, I was also expected to do well at school, so it was lucky that I was so driven.

Even in my family, my mother and father had opposite values systems. My mom was all about openness, transparency, and freedom. But even when I was with her in Canada, I lived by Moroccan standards. Cultural norms are not like a switch that can be turned off and on, therefore, I was never able to experience the free spirit my mother enjoyed. Even as my entire family moved to Canada when I was seventeen, the dichotomies continued. In fact, they actually intensified, which meant I had to double down on my peace-keeping efforts.

Still, my life became full of double standards. A university education was not an option; it was a given. I had to excel at school and establish a career that would give me financial independence and status, yet I couldn't speak up and be assertive or fight for what I believed in. I was expected to behave perfectly and pick the perfect husband, while not being allowed to make the mistakes required to learn. I had to live in Canada, but handle my love life by Moroccan standards. Caught between my father's approval and my desire for agency, it always felt as if I was walking on thin ice. It was suffocating, confusing, and exhausting.

I was, however, allowed to make certain decisions when I fought hard enough. For instance, at the age of eleven, when my family moved to Rabat, I refused to enroll in a French school or another private school. I was adamant that I would go to public school, so my father enrolled me in an all-girls school, where he knew the principal.

Between middle school and high school, I recognized the privilege I had. As soon as teachers knew who my father was, their behavior and attitude would change. In some ways, I enjoyed the attention and respect; however, deep down I knew it was unfair. Thus, I did my best to use that privilege to level the playing field for some of my classmates.

It was heartbreaking to me that no matter what grades I got, I would be guaranteed access to whatever schools I wanted, while so many others who worked very hard, but were from an underprivileged background, felt doomed no matter how hard they tried. As I heard them talk about staying up late to study and worrying about their grades, I wondered what their future would be like. Even listening to our maid describe how she lived—a far cry from our comfortable life—broke my heart.

Studying economics in high school, I had all sorts of questions about how teenagers could work in Canada while in Morocco, many adults could barely seem to find employment. My dad and I had many intellectual conversations, during which I would grill him about why it was that way, and what he could do to change it. "This is unfair. How are these youth supposed to be motivated when they already know they are doomed? There is so much creativity and potential. They are incredibly resourceful and can do amazing things with very little. How can we use that to create better living conditions?" I did not yet have the understanding that, like individuals, each culture has its own history, traumas, evolutionary journey, and most importantly, its own culturally-appropriate ways to grow. Today, I realize that Morocco was a country recovering in a post-colonial era, with many assets, and making its way to economic prosperity in its own way.

As a young person, I often felt helpless and sad, daydreaming of the day I would become a lawyer and bring equality to gender discrimination and class by creating opportunities for additional freedoms and merit-based employment, similar to what I had experienced in Canada.

I had lofty dreams; but first, I was going to live a little. Finally out of the proverbial cage at seventeen, I would venture out into the world and live.

After graduation from high school, I was finally going to move to Montréal. I was longing to live in an environment where no one knew who I was—where I could be free and make my way to law school.

I made sure to get my equivalency in Cégep,[2] got excellent grades, and applied to law school in Montréal. For two years, I lived my dream life. I loved studying sociology and other topics I had not yet been exposed to. Studying anthropology, however, was very difficult. It confronted me with beliefs that were contradictory to some religious ones and created more questions about life in the back of my mind.

Eager to earn my own money, I immediately got a part-time job in a fast food chain five minutes away from school. I also loved dancing and went out clubbing regularly with my friends. I even had a boyfriend; and as my father had declared his only rule was for him to be Muslim, I made sure to only choose a man who would meet his approval.

After two years, we broke up, and I was heartbroken, completely unequipped to deal with the shame of a failed relationship. Not to mention that after such a breakup, any future husband from my culture was likely to be very judgmental of me. Being with a westerner did not feel like an option at this point, and it was very hard for me to be with someone of my own background. Again, I felt like I was on thin ice, trying to negotiate some sense of peace between myself and my cultural conditioning.

Surrendering to the Unfolding

I was an intern at the legal aid clinic, and actively pursuing articling opportunities. Though I got an articling at one of Montréal's top 10 law firms, I suffered from imposter syndrome. I constantly wondered if I was good enough, and it would take years for me to realize it was because I looked nothing like those around me.

Law felt very elitist, and in contrast to the privilege I enjoyed in Morocco, I was just an average girl in Canada. And while I loved it, this meant I had to adjust my experience in a completely different cultural and lived experience to my peers. It was intimidating because I always had the sense of being different. Once again, I didn't fully fit in. Never from one world or the other.

Fortunately, while interning at the legal aid clinic, I met a wonderful mentor, Danielle. She was the first driven, single by choice, independent, and happy woman I'd met; and she had a heart of gold. I confided in her and shared how nervous I was before my interviews. Her down-to-earth presence, openness to cultural nuances, and rigorous legal mentoring were gifts that would stay with me and give me hope in the darkest times. Despite my outstanding performance, the shame, the heartbreak, and imposter syndrome lingered on. But Danielle's guidance and mentoring had also increased my self-confidence and given me a sense of belonging. This duality was a perfect recipe for what would come next.

A friend introduced us. He was Egyptian and Muslim. At first, I wanted nothing to do with him. He seemed arrogant, but he was insistent and he quickly swept me off my feet. I immediately became the center of his world. He wanted to drive me to work and take me out every day, showered me with expensive gifts, and proclaimed his love within two weeks. I was the woman of his dreams, and he was not going to let me go. He had an answer to every objection I had about our relationship moving so fast. My father and family were about to move back to Morocco, and he convinced me it was better to be married than single and alone. "Think about how reassured your dad would be. Couples in our cultures don't even date before marriage, and yet they last for a lifetime," he would say. And like that, in two months, I was getting married.

In August 2001, he was asked to leave the country and wait to get his immigration documents in Egypt. I'd done my due diligence before marrying him, and I was assured it would take no longer than six months. I couldn't leave my husband to go away on his own for six months. That was not okay in our culture according to his father. Being the "good girl," I put my studies on hold for one year and flew to Cairo with him.

9/11 would change everything. As months passed and we received no news of my husband's immigration status, I became increasingly edgy. Despite all of our efforts to move the process forward, six months turned to four and one-half years.

While we waited, my life and marriage took some unexpected and painful turns.

Externally, we looked like a couple in love, enjoying life, quite comfortable financially. Between expensive clothes and diamond jewelry, five-star hotel stays, and regular scuba diving trips to the Red Sea, we appeared to have it all.

But something was amiss, and I couldn't see it... not at first. Growing up privileged, I had inherited the mindset that abuse was linked to poverty, so I believed I could not be going through abuse because it only happened to "others." In fact, the topic was considered taboo in our culture, so it was never addressed openly in a constructive way. Fortunately, life found a way to help me discover the error in these assumptions.

Not sure what I believed or who I believed in, I turned to prayer for answers to the inner and outer conflicts I was experiencing.

Not two weeks later, I turned on the TV to watch my favorite show, Oprah, to find her speaking about the cycle of violence. Her guest had been in an abusive marriage and was sharing her experience. That episode froze the blood in my veins as the distant memory of a social worker's session in Cégep would resurface into my conscious mind. It finally clicked. I was trapped in an abusive marriage. Thousands of miles away from my family. Literally locked away from everyone for days at a time.

My ex-husband had been spiraling out of control, fast; and his behavior was getting more reckless and more dangerous with each passing day. And, like the good girl I had been conditioned to be, I had been doing everything I could to maintain the peace, including smiling when he'd say humiliating things, hiding bruises from physical abuse, and most importantly never saying no to my husband. The ultimate good girl advice I had received, and this is where it had gotten me. I was alone in a foreign country, with no passport for my daughter or myself, not to mention money or access to the outside world. That Oprah episode felt like a jolting yet clear answer to my prayers.

Once I recovered from the shock and horror of my realization, my survival and maternal instincts kicked in. I had not brought a child into the world to teach her this was an acceptable way of living. Despite all odds against me, I was determined to get my daughter out. Through an unbelievable series of events over the next year—an attempt on my life, a heroic father's rescue, a painful separation from my daughter, a staged kidnapping, and an unexpected death to name a few—my daughter and I finally escaped and made it back to Canada.

Throughout that entire journey, I prayed my way to answers and the Universe seemed to continue to deliver them. The right people showed up to confirm my suspicions were true, help me sort through some of the religious and cultural assumptions that were operating in the background, and quite literally rescue me and my daughter.

A few days after our great escape, I was back at university, handing in midterms, rebuilding my life, relieved that my child was back with me. Though I felt broken internally, I kept going. Through it all, I had hope. I was now physically safe, and I had support to continue my studies along with psychological support to begin making sense of the very sudden downward spiral my life had taken.

A few days later, I would hear that my husband had been declared officially missing after a three-day search and rescue operation failed to recover his body from a scuba diving accident. For years, I would remain in judicial limbo. Neither divorced, nor widowed. But I kept going. All I had

Surrendering to the Unfolding

to do was my part, one day at a time. Keep pushing through. Or so I thought.

Finally free of the abusive relationship and done with all the educational requirements, I was called to the Bar in the province of Québec. I was already working for the federal government and thought I had finally made it. In my estimation, I had succeeded at the seemingly insurmountable task of putting my life together in just three years. I had finally pulled it together and even met the young man that is now my husband. I was very nervous about introducing him to my dad, with whom we were living while I finished my bar exams. It was all finally done. I had pulled myself back up by my bootstraps, and the future looked bright.

But the rug got pulled out from under me again. Twenty minutes before my father was supposed to meet my future husband, he announced that he was not going. Without explanations, he stopped talking to me and refused to talk about the incident. Despite my repeated attempts, despite family and friends' attempts. Just like that, I stopped existing for him. The one thing I had gone to great lengths to avoid my whole life had just happened. The paternal anger I always did my best to avoid came crashing to the surface, and in one moment, broke everything, leaving me with the very sense of helplessness and lack of belonging or safety I had worked hard not to feel since childhood.

Once again, the inner landscape would get mirrored externally.

Within a month, I began to suffer at work as the person assigned to be my mentor turned into a total bully. Conditioned to believe I was always at fault, I blamed myself;

for a long time, I thought it was all my fault. After all, my own father had just cut me out of his world, without so much as an explanation. The only explanation my psyche could fathom about my father and my work situation was that I wasn't worthy. Until one day, a colleague let me know I wasn't the only one, and a light bulb went on. What if I wasn't the problem? After all, there was something senseless about these situations where I was blamed, yet never given a reason. At the very least, in a healthy dynamic, I would be given an explanation and an opportunity to correct my behavior. But silence is an effective way of perpetuating control, and I was being given the silent treatment in more than one area. At work, I was stunned to find out that while leadership had pressured me to deal with this problem as if it were my doing, it had failed to do anything about the toxic behavior of this individual several times before. Talk about getting an education on the impact of psychological violence, the hypocrisy of toxic leadership, the systems that enable it, and the implicit culture of silence that keeps it all in place.

Simultaneously, I was awaiting my assignment at the DOJ. Having taken the extremely difficult exams and participated in several interviews, I had finally been selected for a legal position. It was just a matter of a few months, or so I thought. It turns out that being Muslim in Canada, in a post-9/11 world, had its own set of complications. Not only had it held my ex-husband and me up in Egypt for four years longer than expected, but now it was affecting my ability to be employed and live the dream I had worked tirelessly to reach.

Had I been from any other religion, I would have had my clearance before now. However, it would take more than a year for my security clearance to be approved. In the meantime, the new government began cutbacks in public service and my position was cut. Words fail to describe the agony of watching my Canadian-born friends graduate after me and access their positions at the DOJ while I sat waiting, and enduring the soul-crushing impact of systemic racism and toxic leadership.

To be clear, I do understand the fear of the post-9/11 attacks as a human response. However, I am also painfully aware of how it became a justification for racism, how it was spun out of control to cover an entire race rather than some individuals and groups. I am aware of how it has impacted so many of us, Muslim-born, who were just going about our lives, doing our best to navigate the complexities of our cultures of origin, while adopting Canada or a western country as a home.

Perhaps the most painful moment was hearing a colleague allude to the possibility that racism played a role in the way I had been treated by my "mentor." I was so blind to the possibility, so naively believing the ideals of equality I had studied and loved, that I quickly dismissed her. My shock only grew as I began to learn about systemic racism and realized that while I was sworn to uphold the law, a system I so admired, I was simultaneously a victim of it. Would I ever be able to heal from the pain of having succeeded through the same intellectual rigor of legal studies, and still losing access to a position because of others' fear of my race and religion? I had done my part. I had pulled myself up by my bootstraps after the Egypt experience, taken responsibility for my life, maximized the use of every resource I was afforded, and against impossible odds, finished my studies as a single mom, fighting PTSD, and in one of the most difficult disciplines of study. Isn't this what I was supposed to do? Aren't we supposed to reap the rewards of our efforts equally? The painful answer was clearly no. And there were no explanations, no recourse, and nothing in place to mitigate the impact of the security clearance taking so long. Just silence, a long inexplicable wait once again, occasional questions, but never an explanation. Meanwhile, my life was descending into the abyss with ever-increasing panic attacks and illness.

These experiences would give me insights into how we create violence and separation at personal, interpersonal, and systemic levels. The system I had believed in, the hope I had held onto, collapsed under the weight of these experiences. The hopelessness and helplessness resulted in a total breakdown. A sense of loss of all control over my world, and a disillusionment with our systems that unknowingly uphold oppression and inequity. My body and mind were at war with each other and now with the world. The inner conflicts that had been created by culture, religion, and family dysfunction in my early years had become a raging war inside of me as I dealt with similar dynamics in relationships and systems that threatened my future. I could see some of the patterns repeated, but I could not yet see how to reverse them. I felt like despite my best efforts, I kept recreating the patterns of trauma, pain, and dysfunction I was running away from.

That was how I set out to find better pathways to peace—better practices, and tools that would help me to restore peace on the inside and hopefully figure out how to establish it in the world around me too.

And that's exactly what I did over the next nine years because that is how long it took for the small seed of internal wisdom and peace to sprout from the mud of trauma and pain.

Surrendering to the Unfolding

You/We are Not Alone

If you're reading this, it's likely that you have also wondered about your place in the world or felt confined in roles that do not quite fit you, or you may be painfully aware of the unhealthy patterns we live yet feel unable to change them. You may feel like your career is off-sync with your true self, and wonder, *Is this really all I was born for? Paying bills, taking care of others, putting everyone's happiness before my own?* You may even be struggling with living in your culture and feeling like an outsider. But more than anything, you probably feel deeply about finding a way to help everyone around you, and even the global community, thrive.

I realized I was not the only one dealing with wars on the inside and outside when I began interacting with others in the healing space. For the first time in my life, I felt like I was not alone, so relieved to hear that others were asking the same questions. I remember during my first day of coach training when we were asked what brought us there. One of the students said in this shy voice: "I am here because I wonder if there is something wrong with me. The world reacts to my questions weirdly, and I just wonder if it's me." I felt the exact same way. And over the next nine months, I sat with people from all walks of life—from CEOs to housewives, from Asia to North Africa—and I realized no matter our background, we all have a longing to live a good life. To feel fulfilled, to be seen, heard, and valued. To do work that is meaningful, beyond any prestige it can get us. We long to be free and joyful.

I also discovered that we are also highly conditioned in doing what is "right"—in seeking acceptance and love, to the detriment of our needs, well-being, and dreams. We are conditioned to sacrifice ourselves for peace and a false sense of security, and wear that sacrifice as a badge of honor. We are rewarded for that sacrifice—for working long days and hours in positions that drain our energy, only to come home to families that can be demanding and toxic. Or maybe families that we love, while sitting together with invisible walls of disconnection. Feeling alone, though we are together.

I discovered the sad truth to be that self-sacrifice, even in the name of peace, only creates pain, illness, and more disconnection. Then, we go around projecting our pain on each other—blaming each other secretly for our unhappiness and blaming our jobs for the time we put into them and the feeling of being stuck. We blame our governments and corporations for their decisions and actions. In short, we are conditioned to normalize being victims of our ways of life and blame ourselves for questioning if this is really all we are meant to be. Blind to this cultural agreement, we fail to even acknowledge or take responsibility for giving our power away to them—for agreeing to be passive participants in our lives—because being passive is easier in some ways than making the time and diving within to empower ourselves.

I remember sitting in therapy asking how it was possible for a toxic environment to be normal, even glorified. My therapist used to say: "It is crazy-making, but you are not crazy."

Surrendering to the Unfolding

The more I explored, coached clients, and learned new methodologies, the more I found that we are deeply entrenched in unproductive and crazy-making patterns of working hard instead of from a state of flow, of competition instead of collaboration, of exhaustion, of unresolved conflict and self-sacrifice instead of peace. We are taught to normalize cognitive dissonance, rather than seek inner and outer harmony. And we call this success—following a script rather than exploring and embodying the unique expression of who we each came here to be.

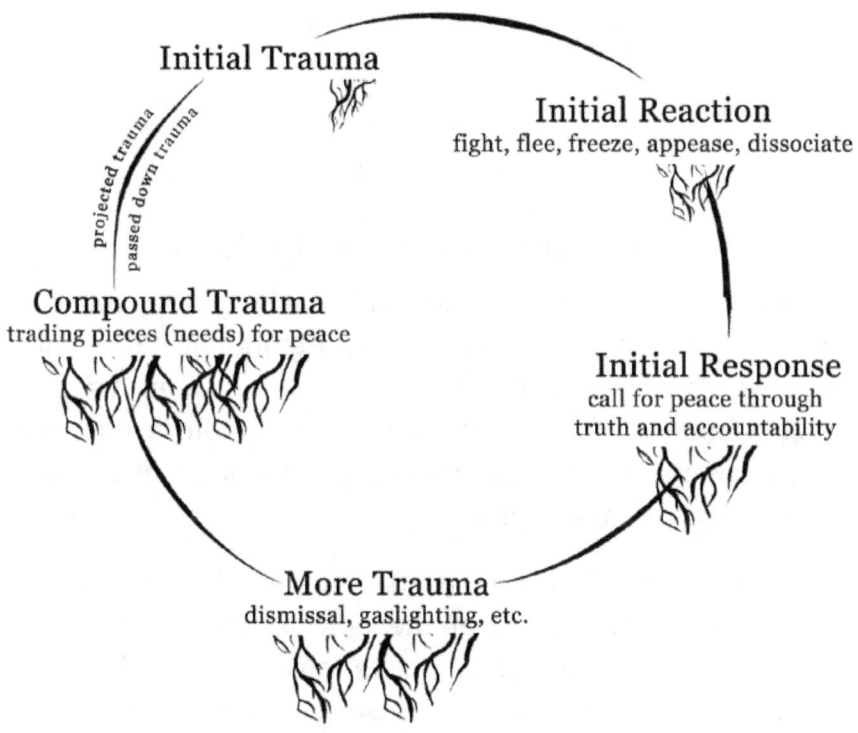

> *Our uniqueness scares us because the individuation process requires letting go. We have not yet recognized that life is about claiming our uniqueness, while being connected to the whole.*

This is also one reason leaders like us feel so lonely. Because we are conditioned to believe we have to do it alone and have all the answers to maintain authority and an image of competence.

There is a Better Way to Peace

I learned through my journey and coaching work that the patterns of behavior causing our discontentment and feelings of separation from others are the same ones keeping us from feeling connected to ourselves, our families, our teams, and our communities. More importantly, I learned that we have the ability to change them.

Through mediation, I realized that we allow conflict to grow and fester, clogging up the judicial systems, and often leaving parties with an incomplete sense of resolution with issues—perpetuating the win-lose model when there are easier, simpler, and more humane ways to tackle conflicts.

Through intercultural training, I learned how culture shapes our lives. I began to understand the beliefs, assumptions, and moral compasses we inherit collectively, and through which we see the world. It became clear how, until they are examined, they remain the real driving forces of our lives.

I remember my first day in law school when the professor declared: "You are here to learn the law. Not justice. If you came here for justice, you are in the wrong place." Yet, my heart had yearned for justice since I was in middle school. And I believe all of our human hearts strive for it. And after years of developing myself as a lawyer, mediator, cross-cultural trainer, coach, facilitator, conscious leader, and human, I believe that justice can only happen if we hear each other, see each other and get to know each other.

As my journey of finding more powerful pathways to peace unfolded, I began to see that the only way to achieve real peace "out there" is to focus on cultivating peace "in here." As I learned the skills and tools I needed to mediate conflict in the world, I turned those practices inward first—negotiating peace between parts of myself, so that I could negotiate peace out there with more of myself participating.

With consistent practice, I found my body's ailments healing, my relationships becoming more fulfilling, and my sense of purpose growing as I began to confront each one of the assumptions that had formed the foundation of my life.

The paradoxes of the journey were baffling at times. The more I stood in my truth, the more I would receive from others. I was pleased to find that while I had been terrified of losing my second husband and daughter if I claimed my needs, our relationships deepened. The more I was assertive and willing to advocate for my needs, the better the quality of life I had, and the more people respected my boundaries.

The more I dared to speak my truth, the better the company I was in. And the more I aligned with my zone of genius and purpose, the more fun my work became, and the more change I was able to make available for others.

I use this approach with family, friends, and colleagues. My clients use it and their relationships become happier, especially their relationship with themselves. The more they release the roles their cultures imposed on them, the more they are able to become authentic and empowered, and the more they inspire others around them to become authentic. The more leaders become aware of their zone of genius, the less they demand their teams to work in non-coherent ways. Instead, they promote well-being and create workplaces where people work from their strengths and passions aligned with their values.

When I met three-time nominee for the Nobel Peace Prize, Dr. Scilla Elworthy, my role model for her pioneering work with policymakers, she confirmed everything I had learned through experience and training: Peace can only be attained if we work toward it and if we make inner peace a priority. Soon after I interviewed her about the link between inner work and leadership outcomes, I became a facilitator and speaker with her organization, the *Business Plan for Peace*. If we are to create a better world, we have to make the connections between well-being, culture, inner power, and systemic inequities, so we can create a world where everyone can live in dignity and peace.

War, whether internal or external, is an outdated paradigm. We are meant for more.

Welcome to your path to more!

Surrendering to the Unfolding

The Purpose and Format of This Book

This is not a "feel-good" easy-to-read, simple self-help book; it is a serious manual for a clearer, more contented, and more fruitful and impactful life. And if you want to change your life, it does demand inner work. Inner work demands planning, focus, application, patience, and determination—and then you have the reward of a more satisfying, calm, fulfilled, and beautiful life in service to your community and the planet. I believe you will find these principles and concepts vital for living and leading in empowered, authentic, uniting, and culturally-adaptable ways, making work an expression of your gifts and a source of joy that is aligned with your values and purpose.

This book presents you with personal stories of my own journey through this framework, inquiries into the beliefs and assumptions that formed us, case studies of clients who have applied these new principles, and practices to help you integrate them into your own life. Of course, the practices suggested require time, implementation, and reflection for integration. The best way to use this book is to read a chapter weekly, apply the specific practices, and then reflect on the suggested practices.

You will also find references to multiple research projects, or other resources that can deepen your understanding and expand your learning. Given the complexity of the topics, each principle could be discussed in a book of its own; and this book is meant to be a guide that opens up a different way of being, a beginning.

I have sought to communicate the universality of our humanity, and as such, address the disempowering beliefs I have encountered across the cultures I have lived in. They may be present to varying degrees; however, the core of the belief is still present because it's human. While the principles speak to the universality of our humanity, I in no way mean to deny our real differences. In fact, my aim is to surface and create connections across our differences in the larger context of our universality. Our work is to discover and live from the sweet spot where our individuality connects us to the whole.

Disclaimers

The principles in this book are ones I learned through personal experience, as well as different frameworks and methodologies. While I share my experiences, especially with medical and mental health issues, I am neither a trained doctor nor therapist; and I do not advocate for ungrounded changes. In fact, I offer my experience as only a source of inspiration and an example that you can explore and adapt to meet your own needs as you learn and integrate these principles.

I invite you, the reader, to find the support of heart-centered and relevant professionals for your own situation, especially if you identify as a highly-sensitive person, or are going through phases of acute illness. I neither offer medical advice nor assessments. You will find that in the resources I share with you, many are from highly-qualified doctors and scientists. Having a caring and well-equipped holistic team is an invaluable resource for meeting our unique needs and healing at all levels. What I speak to in my work is a mindset of presence and empowerment towards our health and every area of our lives, in collaboration with the right professionals to meet our unique individual needs.

I also invite you to make reading this book a journey of self-discovery, even one of self-care. Take your time to read the materials and exercises. Immerse yourself in the explorations, and share them with other like-minded people in your community. Practice the exercises with your teams at work. Keep in mind that these are not one-and-done linear steps, but principles that will support you in unfolding more peace in your life and the world with every day, week, and year that passes. And if you are longing for more guidance or community, join us in the Conscious Togetherness Community where you can adapt an experience congruent with your own personal and collective values, needs, cultural context, and goals.

PS: Some of the names and identities of individuals referred to in case studies have been changed to make sure they are not identifiable.

"We cannot solve our problems with the same level of thinking that created them."

~Albert Einstein~

CHAPTER 1

The Arrogance of Intellect

"You can't go to work tomorrow. You have to go see your family physician." My therapist's words felt far away, as if she was speaking to me from another planet, not the other side of a phone connection.

What? No, this cannot be happening! I screamed internally, not having enough strength in my body to vocalize.

It was a Sunday evening in February 2012, and both my mom and my mother-in-law had been visiting for the weekend. They knew I was struggling, even though I was doing my best to put on a brave face and hide the sinking feeling in my stomach that I was actually getting worse by the minute. Heart racing, head spinning, and visibly shaken, without an apparent trigger, I escaped to my room, reached for the phone, and called my therapist. I never thought I would need her services on Sunday; but there I was, barely able to breathe, on the verge of yet another panic attack.

This is a death sentence. Sitting on the edge of my bed, I saw the first step in the long downward spiral to disability: pain medications, inexplicable symptoms, adverse effects, never-ending doctor visits ending in vague diagnoses and grim prognoses. Having seen hundreds of disability files, all the scenarios in my mind led to permanent disability. Terrified, my body and mind felt frozen.

My worst fear... becoming reality. I had fought with all my might to avoid this day, but my body just could not keep up. I was fighting an invisible force named anxiety, another round with post traumatic stress disorder (PTSD), and chronic pain. In other words, I was back in the cycle of nightmares, a state of constant fear bordering on terror, and sharp stabbing pain throughout my body. And yet, doctors could not pinpoint what was wrong. *This cannot be all in my head, can it? Am I just weak and stupid? Nothing makes sense anymore.*

I had just spent the last two years fighting tooth and nail for the dream life my upbringing had promised me. I had fought to finish my studies, while being a single mom, and getting my health back on track. I had done my part: I had shown up to class every day, studied long hours, and stuck to a workout regimen to strengthen my body and mind. I had followed the doctor's advice diligently. I had sacrificed fun and relaxation to build this new life. I had kept a strict routine six days a week—a routine that would allow me to juggle all of my roles: mother, daughter, sister, employee, citizen... everything but my real self. *Rewards would come after I graduated*, I told myself.

And yet there I was, on the edge of my bed and the precipice of what felt like true disaster. Just when I had gotten all the pieces in order, it felt like the rug was being pulled out from under me.

Isn't this what I was supposed to do? I did my part. Where did I go wrong again?

The Limitations of My Intellect

I was raised to believe that rational thinking, degrees, and studies were the way to success and happiness. And yet there I was, two years after achieving all of that, feeling more broken than before. My health was weaker than before. Any hope that I'd had was replaced with disillusionment, chaos, and despair.

What or who can I trust anymore? My workplace was filled with leaders and colleagues with degrees, and yet they seemed to have no answers to any of life's questions. They were unable to even create a reasonably decent working environment. Then there were the disability files I saw day in and day out that proved that being really smart and accomplished intellectually was no match for the reality of life. And how was I to make sense of having been locked out of opportunities for no reason, and with no answers? Weren't we equal? Isn't that what our laws and constitution are supposed to ensure? The laws and constitution I had been so carefully and enthusiastically studying to uphold?

The truth was that this was just the last bit of evidence I needed to finally give up the illusion that intellect was going to provide me with answers and the happiness for which I had tirelessly worked.

To say I was confused is an understatement, yet fighting was no longer an option. My body was clearly unable to keep up on that path. And so, I did the only thing I could: I surrendered. I listened to my doctors and therapist and stopped. I stopped working; and in doing so, I stopped running away from my deepest fear and stepped right into it. I went on sick leave, for an indeterminate period.

I was going to have to figure this out. If there were different answers at all. The very idea that I would have to find the answers was scary. After all, isn't it every professional's job to have answers in their field? How was I going to find answers to such complex questions: What is the meaning of life? Are our bodies able to heal, or are they meant to be a prison? Why do some of us succeed with little effort while others put huge amounts of effort, only to be met with a different outcome? Why is it that even when we speak, some of us feel invisible? These were the questions that haunted me and weighed on me. It felt like both my sanity and survival were at stake. The first obstacle I had to overcome was the arrogance of intellect. In my quest for answers beyond the modern medical model, I had to surrender to the possibility that some answers lie beyond what my mind could explain. I had to challenge the first disempowering belief so many of us carry. This is when I opened up to the world of healing.

DISEMPOWERING BELIEF #1
We can solve all our problems with our mind.

During childhood, most people are taught to see the intellectual and emotional realms as competing domains in their lives: one can operate *either* from the head *or* the heart. In the West, there is a strong emphasis on the intellectual, rather than emotional aspects of our lives. In fact, it is often idealized as superior. In tandem, we are encouraged to hide

The Arrogance of Intellect

and dismiss our emotions, not to cry when we are hurt, and not to share with others when we are sad or confused. In this rational, linear life model, the mind becomes the master.

The linear life model relies on "left-brain" skills such as critical reasoning, decision-making, and results-orientation while paying scant attention to "right-brain" skills such as empathy and intuition, skills we may not acknowledge, have been exposed to, or learned. Interestingly, in looking at business leaders and executives as models of success, there is increasing acknowledgment that "the science of management, rooted in reasoning and proof points... has served them well, and these capabilities will always be vital. But they are no longer sufficient." Solving the complex problems of today requires a whole-brain approach to leadership in which skills such as inclusivity, coaching, and creative thinking are valued just as much as the understanding of technology, analytics, and critical reasoning. In fact, research has shown a whole-brain approach contributes to 22% higher revenue growth and 34% higher profitability.[3]

So, why then do we continue to rely on the intellect for answers and see emotions as a sign of weakness? We operate under the false premise that thinking is welcome but emotions are not. This, in turn, denies a very basic truth about our biology. Our brain is not only an intellectual center; it is also an emotional center.

Emotions evolved from the environmental challenges that early humans faced, and they result in changes in the brain which, in turn, trigger the nervous system into one of a few states: fight, flee, or freeze. Researchers have actually identified six universal emotions—happiness, disgust, enjoyment, fear, sadness, and anger—that exist in all cultures regardless of how, where, or when people are raised.[4]

Over time, humans began to ignore emotions, choosing to "power" through them and operate despite them, even when their nervous system was sending out alarm signals. This was likely due to a misunderstanding of the function of emotions. In reality, ignoring emotions causes damage to, rather than the strengthening of, our nervous systems.

> The purpose of emotions is to provide feedback on how situations impact us, point us to unmet needs, and support us in adapting strategies to improve our circumstances.

More and more, research is demonstrating the importance of cultivating emotional intelligence and the skills of welcoming, recognizing, naming, and reshaping our emotional states. The idea that emotions indicate weakness is a false narrative, resulting in shame and incompetence in dealing with our feelings. This deficit makes us unable to acknowledge or resolve emotional pain or act on the wisdom of its messages. We are encouraged to push away negative emotions and cover them up. This allows them to fester, amplify, and take over until people find themselves with little choice but to face them. Even then, they do so with feelings of shame and defeat, as if seeking support for emotional pain makes a person weak or flawed. This dangerous dynamic is causing a widespread inability to successfully tackle health and social issues of abuse, depression, anxiety, addiction, overconsumption, and other pressing issues of our time.

The Arrogance of Intellect

Conditioned to use only our minds and think our way through any problem, we become stuck in a constant pattern of working to figure out the answer. When we naturally fail to do so, we think we are stupid. However, the problem is not that we are intellectually incapable. Rather, we are trying to solve the problem from the wrong dimension and without the skills. What does it say when we are proud to attend school to sharpen our intellect, to read books to get smarter, yet we feel ashamed of our inability to create healthy, thriving emotional lives, despite not having any training in doing so?

> *In fact, we are trained not to grow towards emotional maturity.*

As a result, one day, many of us wake up feeling frozen, unable to breathe, feel, or work. Concerned about a heart attack, we may visit the doctor and be told it's just a panic attack and the answer is medication. Or suddenly, we begin snapping at loved ones and colleagues, unable to recognize ourselves in that moment. Although we might feel real regret after, we cannot stop ourselves when the anger takes over. This is inconsistent with what most of us consider smart behavior. And yet, we perpetuate the cycle.

The tragedy of pushing emotions away for years is that it damages our physical, mental, and spiritual health, resulting in individual and collective trauma responses. There is ample scientific evidence proving the linkage between emotional states and physical illness. Gabor Mate, physician and author, demonstrates the link between stress and illness in his book, *When the Body Says No: Understanding the Stress-Disease Connection*.[5] David Servan-Schreiber, a clinical professor of psychiatry at the University of Pittsburgh School of Medicine, explores in-depth the link between emotions and illness in his book, *The Instinct to Heal: Curing Depression, Anxiety and Stress Without Drugs and Without Talk Therapy*.[6]

To recognize how emotions compound over time, imagine you have an unseen, emotional "storage bin" in your body. Every time an emotion remains unprocessed, it goes into this storage bin. This bin is not only never emptied; you don't even acknowledge its existence—you just turn away from it every time you begin to sense it. This is largely what drives addictions such as food, sex, alcohol, shopping, and gambling. These distractions enable one to numb those inconvenient emotions. Then with emotions trapped in your body and no ability to process them, your mind gets hijacked when strong emotions are triggered.

You become unable to regulate your brain when it goes into an instinctive fight, flight, freeze, appease, or dissociate response. Aside from rendering you inefficient at handling your emotions, this process also causes suffering. Most people are so conditioned to tolerate and normalize this suffering that they believe hiding and denying their emotional pain is a sign of strength. The worst part is that this desensitization process makes them unable to feel contentment, ease, and peace, making them victims to suffering.

In my work with clients, this desensitization shows up as unfulfilled relationships, an inability to speak up, imposter syndrome, problems with authority figures, constant conflict, avoidance, illness, inability to access creativity, and in myriad other ways. At its extreme, unacknowledged emotions compound and accumulate until they reach the threshold of debilitating trauma. Trauma is generally misunderstood as a particularly debilitating event. However, trauma can come from a combination of micro-traumas. We may not even remember the events because our memory will try to block them; however, the memory of the trauma remains in our body. We find our response is disproportionate and label ourselves as weak. It is important to recognize here that, at this point, it is no longer the actual events that cause the loss of emotional balance, but rather, the hidden emotional memory they trigger, one that we are likely unaware of.

In my own life, I spent years recovering from trauma and anxiety. There was a time when for months and months, I would be working or doing the most mundane tasks when suddenly, something would feel wrong. An insurmountable fear would grip me. My heart would race, my knees weaken, my palms sweat, and I would struggle to breathe. I wanted to run away from where I was at that moment. What was happening to me? Over the following months, I would be unable to sleep. I'd be in the middle of a meal and suddenly feel unable to stomach another bite. I'd be out with friends or family and suddenly feel like I needed to return home. For a couple of years, I felt great shame and confusion as I battled to understand what was happening. I felt like I was standing in quicksand, unable to move or escape these feelings. Through a long recovery process, I became aware of the function the brain plays in emotional regulation and, more specifically, how the fear response gets triggered. This understanding helped me become very skilled at regulating it and, eventually, releasing trauma from my body.

While the fight or flight response mechanism kept our ancestors safe in the face of physical threats such as tigers, our bodies generate the same response to emotional threats. Both these perceived threats and our reactions are further conditioned by our upbringing, culture, and gender. Research shows that for a young boy, a fight response shows up as aggression, a flight response as defiance, and a freeze response as resistance. In contrast, for a young girl, a fight response will show up as fainting, a flight response into dissociation, and a freeze response as compliance.[7]

This is likely because in most cultures, boys are socialized to be "tough" and rewarded for risk-taking; hence, the rebellious response. For boys and men, crying or acknowledging pain is perceived as weakness. Girls, on the other hand, are socialized to feel their emotions to the extent of inaction. Boys are labeled as courageous for risk-taking and not demonstrating signs of emotion or empathy, while girls are rewarded for taking care of others and being passive. This is the reason many women struggle with being assertive while most men struggle with crying and empathizing. These actions become "threats" and when the brain perceives a threat, it mobilizes the body for fight or flight. If you see a fist coming at you, your brain will make you react, raise your arm, and hit in return, or move your body to avoid the punch. But what happens when the threat is not physical—when instead, it is the invisible fear of speaking your opinion or being perceived

The Arrogance of Intellect

as weak for crying? The emotion gets stuck, turning into a painful dormant memory in your "emotional storage bin."

How does the brain decide what is a threat? In a nutshell, any past experience that caused you pain and remained unprocessed will create a fight or flight stress response, and your brain will instinctively try to shield you from it. Think of the first time you were punished for crying, or told "boys don't cry," or "good girls don't get loud, talk back, or do that type of work." Though each situation is nuanced, these generalizations indicate patterns across many cultures. The accumulation and intensity of such experiences create an inability to handle the emotion attached to this internalized message and experience, a feeling of overwhelm, and a sense of losing control.

The same dynamic happens with CEOs in boardrooms as it does at any dinner table around the world. The impact is always a loss of internal safety, internal power, and disconnection from others. Once the emotions are processed, new dynamics become possible. The mind can find harmony with the same experience, and the body returns to a state of balance. This is how we move from frustration, pain, and powerlessness to empowerment and self-regulation.

When we find ourselves repeating a pattern we dislike, we need to inquire deeper into the source of our actions. The solution will emerge as we engage with the problem from a different dimension.

You may also notice that two people can experience the same event yet react completely differently. This points to the individual ways that we relate to experiences and process them, beyond our conditioning. Consider how your culture has played a role in your relationship to emotions from a young age. What did you learn about emotions as a child? How did your parents respond when you were frightened? Or when you cried?

Breaking the Cycle

A client of mine, let's call him Anthony, came into our session with this exact problem. At the age of 42, he was struggling with his strong reaction to certain situations. He didn't know why it happened, and he felt unable to stop it despite how much he hated the loss of control. He was distraught because he couldn't see it coming until it was too late: "Sometimes, I just get upset and confront the other person aggressively. Afterward, I end up feeling regretful and upset because I hurt them. This is not working, but I don't know why it happens or what to do about it. I don't even get what I wanted in the first place."

During our work, we discovered this reaction occurs whenever he thought he was being treated unfairly. This thought triggered a strong reaction that made him lash out at any person he perceived was treating him inequitably. After spending time compassionately inquiring into this dynamic, we found an intense feeling of sadness and helplessness underlying the trigger.

The Arrogance of Intellect

On the surface, his actions seemed aggressive. Yet deeper exploration revealed this aggressive behavior was, in fact, fueled by intense and overwhelming feelings of hopelessness and fear.

As we continued exploring, a memory from Anthony's childhood surfaced. He had suffered the unexpected loss of his mother. The pain was overwhelming. It felt so unfair to lose his mother as a young boy. The loss was so sudden, it left him with a bitter taste of unfairness. Watching friends grow up with their mothers, play with them at the park, share life with them, and feel safe and cared for in their presence created the belief that life was unfair and he needed to fight for survival. To him, the emotional memory of the loss, though at a subconscious level, was so overbearing that he couldn't contain his emotions when this feeling was triggered; and it turned to aggression instead.

Through our work, he was able to feel the unprocessed grief from the passing of his mother, the loss of the broken connection, and the years that felt unlived. In doing so, a new pathway opened up for a different response. Anthony eventually understood that he was safe, even when emotions became intense. Once he became aware of this dynamic, he learned to catch himself when feelings of hopelessness surfaced and choose to respond differently.

Ultimately, this meant that he was able to recognize that the other person was not oppressing him as he had thought, but rather that he was feeling triggered. Self-management and self-inquiry practices gave him the ability to step out of autopilot, breathe, process, and recover. This change helped him remain in relationships that would have been lost in the past.

This is how Anthony moved from feeling like a victim to an Empowered Self when he was faced with this trigger. After recognizing the trigger, he learned to calm and control his brain and move from reaction to response.

This is the cyclical process through which you can move from disempowering dynamics and mindsets to more empowering ones.

Everyone has the ability to move past triggers and become powerful and peaceful, even in the face of suffering. This is cultivated through a set of practices that enable the development of your inner witness, which helps you create an internal space where you can catch emotions between trigger and reaction. This is ultimately how you disrupt the pattern. Any mindful practice will strengthen your inner witness, and you can find one that activates your inner observer as quickly and efficiently as possible. Most of my clients find a huge benefit in taking up meditation and journaling as a starting point.

Several research studies confirm the effectiveness of meditation and mindful practices in calming the amygdala and moving the body from a stress response (fight, flight, or freeze) to a more relaxed response where the heart rate drops back to normal, the stress markers lower, and muscle tension eases up. Changes have also been found in the hippocampus, providing access to improved emotional control. Research participants self-reported a greater ability to cope, reduced negative thoughts, and increased self-esteem.[8]

Learning to use our minds optimally, rather than compulsively, and connect with the wisdom of our emotions and bodies helps us regulate our emotional states and expands our repertoire of resources for a better quality of life and empowered living.

> *PRINCIPLE #1*
> *Our body, emotions, and intuition hold wisdom that contributes to solving problems holistically.*

Practice: Going Beyond the Intellect

1 - Meditation

Get started in a simple and effective way!

Many clients ask me how to meditate. With a multitude of options out there, they feel lost and are also concerned about doing it wrong. Being a trauma survivor, I experimented with many types of mindful practices, which has allowed me to support each client in quickly identifying the best practice for them.

Here is some simple advice to begin your practice: recognize that even as you are embarking on a practice that allows you to experience your "being," your mind has become so conditioned in "doing" that performance anxiety may keep you away from starting. Make a conscious decision to begin, and give yourself permission to jump in.

Then, find a meditation that calms you, whether it is a guided meditation with simple soothing background music or a self-guided meditation where you keep your focus on your breath. Whatever feels right, try it.

In fact, I invite you to identify a meditation you like today and challenge yourself to meditate daily for 10 days. Keep notes on your daily experience in meditation and throughout your day. After 10 days, assess what has shifted. You will find a great resource at the link below to explore some guided meditations by the Mindfulness Center at University of California in Los Angeles. Through their online meditations, classes, or the UCLA Mindful app, you will find different lengths and intentions, including ones for difficult emotions, for sleep, for breath, or even just a short three-minute one to start.[9]

Once you find one that works for you, do it every day. It is not the length of the practice, but the regularity of it, that will make the biggest impact. Begin with three minutes a day if you cannot commit longer periods of time. Most importantly, do not put undue pressure on yourself to meditate to stop your thoughts. As a beginner, allow yourself to simply watch what is happening inside as you sit quietly with yourself. Notice your thoughts, physical sensations, restlessness, sleepiness, or whatever comes up. Put your focus on *simply noticing*. Whatever is present for you in that moment, let it be and notice it as if you're watching a movie. No judgment, no labels, just noticing. Over time, and with regular practice, your inner witness will strengthen and your ability to shift from reaction to response will increase.

2 - Journaling

When you encounter a situation that triggers you emotionally, and find yourself unsure why you reacted the way you did, take a pause, and journal. Allow yourself to write down how you were feeling, and all your thoughts unfiltered. You will likely be surprised how much new insight you can find to what drives your behaviour.

It Takes Time

It took a long time for me to realize that my intellect was only going to take me so far and that without a holistic approach, I was going to stay on the precipice of illness, despair, and permanent disability.

But that Sunday, by the time I hung up the phone with my therapist, I knew she was right. No amount of help from my mom or mother-in-law, or anyone else for that matter, was going to stabilize me. I had reached the end. Only I could rescue myself.

I needed to dive deep into my emotional storage bin and start processing what was there, but how would I do it?

> "Vulnerability is our most accurate measure of courage."
> ~Brené Brown~

CHAPTER 2

The Power of Vulnerability

After nine months of intense healing work, therapy, and many doctor visits, I was finally ready to go back to work. I initiated the conversations with my union representative, my doctor, and my insurance company to create a return-to-work plan.

Filled with a complicated set of enthusiasm and terror at the idea of going back, I attended to the war with fear waging inside.

I'd have to face these people again. *What if I can't take the pressure and crumble? What if I can't hold my boundaries again? What if my body betrays me and my voice starts shaking? I'll look like a loser. What if I find out I really cannot work at all? It can't be. There has to be something I am capable of doing.*

I worried about the impact on those I love. *What if I disappoint my husband and he leaves me? What would I be teaching my daughter about facing adversity if I don't go back?* I couldn't bear the thought of her seeing me quit without having tried everything I knew how.

I wondered what would happen if I actually made it. *What if I pull it off? Maybe and just maybe someday I can look back and be proud of this step. I'll never know if I don't try. And I will always blame myself if I don't give it my best shot.*

I'd sit by the waterfront at the marina near our house for hours, caught between daydreaming and rehearsing the nightmare scenarios. But deep down, I knew the only right next step for me was to go back. No matter how much my mind tried to scare me, my heart kept pulling me to go back. So once more, I planned for the worst, hoped for the best, and plunged into the unknown.

It had taken a huge amount of vulnerability to swallow my pride and accept that going back felt like the right thing to do, even though every cell in my body felt ready to run for the hills. And it took a lot of courage to face the possibility of failing in my return to work. I was about to find out if the strengthening process had been sufficient or if I was going to fall apart again.

These questions and fears haunted me as I picked up the phone to talk with the insurance representative; and as she was asking probing questions, I felt overwhelmed with emotion.

She could hear my tears through the phone. "Are you sure you are able to go back?"

Are you kidding me? I remember thinking. *I am putting my best effort to face a deeply traumatic past. And I do not have an answer to your question. However, I am willing to do the work to find out. At the risk of failing. Having no prospect of being gainfully employed or enjoying life at the age of thirty-three is not the life I signed up for.*

I wanted to scream: "Lady, your job is to help me figure out *how* I can make this work, not be skeptical because I am crying."

But being the good girl I was, I politely replied, "It is really hard to go back, and I know I may fail, but I really want to give it my best shot."

> ### DISEMPOWERING BELIEF #2
> Vulnerability is weakness.

We all experience adversity in life. How we handle these unexpected difficulties both mentally and emotionally can either help us become stronger and more resilient beings or hobble us and stunt our personal growth, potentially making us more susceptible to disease later in life.[10]

Adversity primes some people to move forward, confident that despite setbacks, they have the tools, mindset, and support to overcome them. For them, adversity can become an experience of strength and proof that they are able to weather difficult circumstances, take stock, and maneuver ahead, perhaps even grow from the situation.

For others, the trauma from adversity can be deeply damaging, leaving them feeling weak, ashamed, despairing, or unworthy. The experience becomes a dark secret, difficult to share with others, and even more difficult to confront within oneself. People who internalize these difficulties often project self-blame or a sense that they deserve the situation they are in. They become scared to reach out for support and fear judgment and rejection should they share their experience with others. This adversity eventually gives rise to a limiting pattern, a hurdle that consciously or subconsciously seeps into every aspect of one's physical, emotional, and mental life.

The limiting belief that acknowledging challenges or failures makes us weak keeps us from stepping into our healing. This inability to share with others keeps us wounded or in denial, unable to accept important aspects of ourselves, and leaves our body and inner self out of alignment. It's akin to a battle within—bodily sensations become numbed, actions may not align with intuition, and the voice in our head denies the feeling in our gut. This disempowering belief that vulnerability is weakness ultimately prevents us from healing.

But what is vulnerability?

Vulnerability takes two shapes. The broadly acknowledged definition is one that deals with our interactions with others. According to the Oxford Dictionary, vulnerability means the quality or state of being exposed to the possibility of being attacked or harmed, either physically or emotionally. Vulnerability occurs passively in children who are unable to feed, clothe, or care for themselves; and so are in a naturally vulnerable state if left unattended. For adults, vulnerability is more commonly about emotional self-protection.

Consider this. When asked how you are, how often do you automatically find yourself saying, "I'm fine," even when you are not? We have become socially conditioned to respond this way, even with close friends or family, and even when it simply isn't true. Over time, we learn to fear that acknowledging the truth of how we feel or what we are going through may result in blame, judgment, or rejection. This leaves us unable to be open, share our lived experiences, and acknowledge our emotional welfare.

The second aspect of vulnerability is one that often occurs when a damaging experience becomes internalized and we are unable to be vulnerable with ourselves. We resist acknowledging or being honest with ourselves about the truth of how we feel or think. As time passes, we become detached from our authentic selves, potentially leading to a host of ailments that manifest themselves physically or mentally such as anxiety, depression, or abuse. This often leads to numbing practices like overeating, procrastination, avoidance, and many others. Even practices such as exercising can be a numbing strategy when done excessively.

We have been socially conditioned to believe that vulnerability is a weakness that allows others to take advantage of us. This bias exists due to the false notion that it is a "dog eat dog" world. We maintain a facade of strength as a protective mechanism to avoid appearing like a "loser." We want to appear tough rather than vulnerable, so others will respect our projected strength, even if it's not felt. Subconsciously, we fear that if we acknowledge we are not doing well or that we don't have certain answers, it means we are frail and incapable of taking care of ourselves, unable to be an "adult," stupid, or less worthy than others. We fear that even if we open ourselves up, we still won't have the answer or the remedy to our problems.

> *The real problem is that it simply isn't true. Vulnerability, in fact, opens a whole new world for each of us.*

In Brené Brown's famous Ted Talk about *The Power of Vulnerability*, she talks about being vulnerable to another person as a personal acknowledgment of "uncertainty, risk, and emotional exposure."[11] Within that acknowledgment lies the idea that each of us is stronger than we realize and we need to fail and have the ability to learn and grow from those failures. This acknowledgment that we are continuously growing and never a finished product means it is okay to not have all the answers. This helps us to build the understanding and acceptance that we are indeed human, and thus have emotions and continuous cycles of growth in every area. Life is a journey, unfolding moment to moment, rather than a destination with pre-set markers such as degrees, job titles, levels of income, and social standing.

> *Vulnerability assures us of a sense of belonging.*

As inherently social creatures, opening up about fears and our lived experiences can breed intimacy, build compassion, and inspire others to be authentic. On a larger scale, we acknowledge our shared humanity. For too long, society has been signaling that vulnerability is a weakness. Reclaiming ourselves and our society hinges on being vulnerable. Only through being vulnerable can we truly build our character and sense of self, normalize our human experiences, and live authentically.

Vulnerability, however, does not include oversharing or sharing everything with everyone. It must be purposeful. In truth, not everyone deserves to hear our story. Selective vulnerability, in which we carefully choose who to open up to, enables deeper connection. The best way to think of vulnerability is a skill we develop. Since the biggest block to vulnerability is shame, it is very important to develop this skill gradually, in a way that does not leave us feeling overexposed, or raw in a damaging way.

The most important person to be vulnerable with is oneself. We alone hold the key to our life, and even well-intentioned loving friends and family will not necessarily have the right answers for us. They may offer compassion, guidance, and support, yet the real answers lie solely within us.

Opening up to our own vulnerability requires us to overcome our inner critic, which takes courage and discernment. Silencing our inner critic requires strength, patience, and persistence. It will not happen easily and some days will be harder than others. Yet with this intention and practice comes the reward of an authentic connection with oneself and others, ultimately increasing our ability to meet our own needs.

My own practice of vulnerability is one that has rewarded me greatly, with deeper relationships and more meaningful experiences.

A couple of years into my healing journey and a few months after I moved to South Korea, I had committed to meeting a woman to whom I had recently been introduced. As an expatriate, our social circle changed constantly, and connecting with like-minded people was important. Although I wanted to get to know her better, I wasn't feeling up to meeting that day as I was feeling very vulnerable.

I was aware that when I felt anxious, I could come across as withdrawn and potentially cold to people who did not know me. Friends back home, who knew me well, did not take it personally or judge me when I was feeling anxious. But feeling vulnerable and fragile in a new environment wasn't a prospect I was thrilled about. My need for emotional safety was in conflict with my need for connection.

After some consideration, I decided to meet with her despite my reservations. When she asked me how I was, I honestly admitted things were not going well that day, that I was feeling generally anxious, and that I know that I can come across as withdrawn when in this state. I even requested that if she should notice it that she not take it personally. In sharing, I knew I was taking an emotional risk, so I only shared the part I was comfortable with, even though it was vulnerable. At that point in my life, I was not interested in spending time with people if I needed to pretend all was great. While this was a risk, I saw it as a potentially revealing interaction about whether this person could be a good friend.

To my surprise, she shared that though she did not personally suffer from anxiety, she had family members who did and understood what it meant. She even asked me if she could do anything to help, and I responded that simply being able to name it was enough for me. We ended up having a lovely lunch and our families went on to create a friendship that has lasted the tests of time and distance.

> This is one benefit of vulnerability—it allows us to build authentic relationships where we can show up fully and be our messiest and best selves at the same time.

Breaking the Cycle

One of my early clients came to me through the referral of a friend who had found her life purpose while working with me and was much happier and at ease with herself. This woman was initially unsure whether I could also support her, but she was willing to explore the possibility.

On our first call, she shared with me that she was not attracted to the gender she was expected to be by society, which caused her shame and guilt. As a result, she was self-conscious in social situations and lived in constant fear of rejection. After years of hiding from her truth, she had finally decided to face this buried pain that was torturing her internally. During the sessions that followed, I helped her explore the source of her guilt and shame, and she found herself remembering an abusive situation she had experienced in her family. As a result, she formed the belief that she was not worthy of love or compassion. As we continued to inquire and be curious with that wounded part of her, she readied herself to release the pain and trapped energy of that experience. We closed that particularly intense session with the agreement that the client would commit to self-care over the following days.

A few days later, I received a message from her in which she shared that she had experienced a huge release, followed by a burst of energy. She had even resumed painting, something she had been unable to do for years. I was impressed and inspired by her ability to face her own truth and courageously inquire into the source of her pain. In that moment, I realized the direct link between our creativity and the buried pain we carry. The simple act of facing her pain and releasing it allowed her to access her creative spark again after five years of wondering why she was not able to paint anymore.

A few sessions later, deeper exploration connected her with the intuition that the time for her to be honest had come. She was no longer willing to hide and live in shame. Despite her fears, she decided that she was ready to share her truth and did so authentically with her staff and colleagues. Although sharing made her feel extremely vulnerable, it connected her with her true inner strength and self-acceptance. In this case, the risk paid off.

The result was a deepening of her connection with others. She finally felt that she belonged and experienced more freedom and ease in her work relationships. She went from being scared of being judged to being promoted several months later; because she was able to act more authentically, express her ideas, access her creativity, and communicate more openly and assertively. This is the power of vulnerability.

> PRINCIPLE #2
> Vulnerability, with self first, is essential to connection.

Vulnerability Pays Big Dividends

Though I was scared of returning to the same environment after my sick leave, I had learned through exposure therapy that it was a way to recover. And somewhere deep down, it was a way to reclaim my lost dignity.

It would take incredible amounts of vulnerability and courage to walk back into that environment, manage all of my triggers, and stick to my intentions to respond differently and shift the dynamic that had been creating such chaos and pain in my life.

But it was the only way, and I knew it.

Practice: Building Self-awareness and Emotional Resilience

Naming Your Emotions

In both personal and leadership work, one of the foundational pieces in developing self-awareness, emotional competence, and resilience is becoming aware of your emotional state and being vulnerable with yourself. A powerful practice to develop these skills is learning to name your emotions in the moment. Though we have six broad categories of emotion, going deeper into the nuances at the initial stages of this learning process is important. Much like learning a new language, it requires time, practice, and attention to detail. I see many clients who begin their explorations with the belief that they are aware of their emotions, yet this process consistently brings them to a deeper recognition of themselves, their emotional triggers, and their needs.

Over the next week, I suggest you carry the following lists of emotions with you and occasionally check in with yourself to name your emotions, especially when you feel triggered.[12]

Identifying your emotions is the first step in learning to regulate them. Over time, you will recognize patterns in your emotional states and learn to shift them much faster.

Leaning into your emotions may make you feel vulnerable, especially with those emotions deemed "negative." While people have a tendency to categorize emotions as good and bad, and therefore wanted and unwanted, the reality is emotions are nothing more than messages. Although you might find internal resistance when diving into "negative" emotions, acknowledge the resistance and make a decision to name the emotion. Each time you do this, you will activate your courage and feel more connected to yourself. Notice your bodily sensations when you finally name the correct emotion. You will likely find your body relaxes as it realizes that its message has been received and acknowledged.

To practice appreciation and gratitude for your life, I highly recommend doing this exercise daily, for both positive and difficult situations. I find this approach allows for feeding the positive in your life while releasing the difficult, bringing more ease and grace to the journey.

Difficult Emotions[13]

ANGER

Enraged
Furious
Incensed
Indignant
Irate
Livid
Outraged
Resentful

ANNOYANCE

Aggravated
Dismayed
Disgruntled
Displeased
Exasperated
Frustrated
Impatient
Irritated
Irked

AVERSION

Appalled
Contempt
Disgusted
Horrified
Repulsed
Confused
Baffled
Bewildered
Dazed
Hesitant
Lost
Mystified
Perplexed
Puzzled
Torn

DISCONNECTION

Alienated
Aloof
Apathetic
Bored
Cold
Detached
Distant
Distracted
Indifferent
Numb
Removed
Uninterested
Withdrawn

DISQUIETNESS

Agitated
Alarmed
Discombobulated
Disconcerted
Disturbed
Perturbed
Rattled
Restless
Shocked
Startled
Surprised
Troubled
Turbulent
Turmoil
Uncomfortable
Uneasy
Unnerved
Unsettled
Upset
Embarrassed
Ashamed
Chagrined
Flustered
Guilty
Mortified
Self-conscious

The Power of Vulnerability

Difficult Emotions [14]

FATIGUE

Beat
Burned Out
Depleted
Exhausted
Lethargic
Sleepy
Tired
Weary
Worn Out

FEAR

Apprehensive
Dreading
Foreboding
Frightened
Mistrustful
Panicked
Petrified
Scared
Suspicious
Terrified
Wary
Worried

PAIN

Agony
Anguished
Bereaved
Devastated
Grief
Heartbroken
Hurt
Lonely
Miserable
Regretful
Remorseful

SADNESS

Depressed
Dejected
Desperate
Despondent
Disappointed
Discouraged
Disheartened
Forlorn
Gloomy
Heavy-hearted
Hopeless
Melancholic
Unhappy
Wretched
Tense
Anxious
Cranky
Distressed
Distraught

Edgy
Fidgety
Frazzled
Irritable
Jittery
Nervous
Overwhelmed
Restless
Stressed Out

VULNERABILITY

Fragile
Guarded
Helpless
Insecure
Leery
Reserved
Sensitive
Shaky

YEARNING

Envious
Jealous
Longing
Nostalgic
Pining

Happy Emotions[15]

AFFECTION

Compassionate
Open-hearted
Sympathetic
Tender
Warm
Engaged
Absorbed
Alert
Curious
Engrossed
Enchanted
Entranced
Fascinated
Interested
Intrigued
Involved
Stimulated

CONFIDENCE

Empowered
Open
Proud
Safe
Secure

HOPE

Expectant
Encouraged
Optimistic

EXCITEMENT

Amazed
Animated
Ardent
Aroused
Astonished
Dazzled
Eager
Energetic
Enthusiastic
Giddy
Invigorated
Lively
Passionate
Surprised
Vibrant

GRATITUDE

Appreciative
Moved
Thankful
Touched

INSPIRATION

Amazed
Awed
Joyful
Amused
Delighted
Glad
Happy
Jubilant

HAPPINESS

Exhilarated
Blissful
Ecstatic
Elated
Enthralled
Exuberant
Radiant
Rapturous
Thrilled

PEACE

Calm
Clear-headed
Comfortable
Centered
Content
Equanimous
Fulfilled
Mellow
Quiet
Relaxed
Relieved
Satisfied
Serene
Still
Tranquil
Trusting
Refreshed
Enlivened
Rejuvenated
Renewed
Rested
Restored
Revived

Gathering My Courage

What the insurance representative didn't know was that for the last few months of sick leave, conversations with my therapist were leading me to the realization that I had been living completely disconnected from my true self. My work had been not only uninspiring and mundane but downright toxic. Though I believed our bodies could heal, I was confronted daily with files of individuals whose only prospect for income was to be declared disabled. Though I believed in the Law and my ability to help others with it, I had come face-to-face with inequality as I grappled with questions about why my clearance hadn't come through.

Most importantly, I was now face-to-face with the repeated pattern in my life: attracting toxic individuals into my life and giving them my power. I could finally see that because they were in positions of power, culturally speaking, I was trusting them blindly despite their behavior, which continually proved they were not worthy of trust. I was believing their words and the position of authority they were in over my own experience and that of others. I let their behavior go on, believing I had no other choice. One thing had become clear to me. Though I looked like the victim in these scenarios, I had been an active participant in them. I had learned in my childhood to be a good girl—to stay quiet to keep the peace. This meant I had not developed the capacity to be assertive or to hold my boundaries. Instead, I had learned to tolerate toxicity and see it as normal—at the cost of my own health and life.

"I have to go back and face this," I had told my therapist. "If I keep running away, I will likely run into the same dynamic."

"What is necessary to change a person is to change his awareness of himself."
~Abraham Maslow~

CHAPTER 3

The Freedom of Choice

"Paula, if what is best for me is to leave, I will not ask anyone for permission. I am telling you that I came back to face the events I suffered here, not asking you for permission. The only choice you get is whether you will help me do what is right for me or whether I will have to do it on my own."

My manager looked at me, stunned at my response to her statement that I was considered too valuable to the workplace and would likely not be supported if I asked to be let go. The stakes were so high for me with this return to work that I was exploring all of my options, and when she made that statement, something visceral moved in me, almost like a mother protecting her child.

I had never planned to say those words, and it was certainly uncharacteristic of me to speak so forcefully and with such boldness to someone in a position of authority. But being "nice" was clearly overrated, so it was time to get real.

In the months that I had been recovering, I had decided to value self-care, advocate for my own needs, and face conflict head-on. I had learned not to trust by default that leadership had employees' best interests at heart; I'd recognized the need to take responsibility for my health, and well-being, even if it meant saying *no*. And especially when it meant saying *no*. Even so, I had no idea what the response would be.

But I was determined to no longer leave important decisions about my life and career in the hands of "leaders." I was committed to giving myself the freedom to explore and choose what was right for me. And I was committed to creating a career that aligns with my values, and what matters to me.

> DISEMPOWERING BELIEF #3
> We are at the mercy of other people's actions.

One of the biggest misconceptions I encounter in working with clients is the idea that our feelings are triggered by other people's actions. As a result, we believe that our reactions are caused by other people's actions too. We are so conditioned into these beliefs that we do not even recognize that we are simultaneously blaming others for how we feel *and* giving them our power. We can see this behavior exhibited as early on as childhood. Have you ever seen a child hit someone because they are upset that they took away their toy?

As a child, it is difficult to recognize that we have been triggered and that we could simply ask for our toy back. We go on as adults perpetuating the same behavior. Instead of naming our emotions and owning our unmet needs and desires, we blame our family members, friends, colleagues, or culture for our unhappiness.

Our culture raises us with a belief system of what we can or cannot do, what is and is not acceptable behavior, what

The Freedom of Choice

we deserve and should have, or what others deserve but we do not. Of course, not all cultural beliefs and narratives are disempowering. However, the disempowering beliefs become like an invisible ceiling of what we believe we can reach for in life as a result of our gender, our identity, status, or any other defining characteristic. Most people hold these limiting beliefs as true for themselves, and they become the unconscious lenses through which they see the world and make sense of it. They are negative because they are not true, yet believing them causes both pain and inaction. These beliefs can have a significant impact on our life, holding us back from joy, personal growth, and achieving our potential and dreams.

The difficulty in recognizing these beliefs is that we constantly see evidence that reinforces them in our daily life, especially when they are the majority's beliefs. We usually begin to question them only when we go through serious life events that shake us, or when exposed to a completely different way of being that confronts our preconceived notions of how life works. Cross-cultural experiences are often a catalyst for such reflection. We meet people who hold very different, sometimes opposing, beliefs about the world and what's right or not; and we begin to see there are multiple valid perspectives about many facets of life. In the past decade, there has been an increasing openness to recognizing these beliefs as a collective, as we are seeing with the increased awareness of gender identities, or the impact of dominant identities on marginalized identities in society.

The biggest difficulty with limiting beliefs is that they create an invisible barrier to how far we can stretch in life and what we can have as a result. For example, there was a time when the generalized, collective belief was that it was impossible for people to fly. It took the Wright brothers to question and challenge that belief in order to change it. Until that point, travel had this invisible boundary—it could only happen by other means.

What might this look like for us in one's personal or professional life? Think about the man raised in a culture that perceives a man crying as a sign of weakness and worthy of ridicule. As a result, these men bottle up emotion and harden, believing they have no other choice. The limiting belief that they cannot cry causes them to hold on to a lot of emotional pain and resort to numbing their feelings in other ways to maintain a masculine image and, therefore, be worthy of respect according to the cultural norm. Unfortunately, the cost is high. They often feel internally disconnected from their family members and may even lose touch with who they are in this process, going through life wearing masks that don't really fit them.

While the limiting belief is collective and stems from the culture, breaking through it is a personal experience that happens as the man is able to let go of the importance of the masks and perfect image inherited from their culture. Instead, they become able to see the strength and beauty in being emotionally tuned in, and competent. This gives them the ability to regulate the emotions that cause them pain, allowing them access to true joy, connection, and empathy.

Of course, breaking through culturally limiting beliefs can be costly; it defies the prevailing narrative and can feel isolating. However, when navigated with the proper tools and support, it is possible to reconcile the needs of the individual and

The Freedom of Choice

society, rather than continue operating under a false zero-sum narrative where the needs of one outweigh the other.

Another example I often encounter is the belief that we cannot have a career we love and get paid well. We may be surrounded by many people who have the same belief; so when we see others who have created a career they love and that also pays well, we may call it luck or say they are well off and can afford to be picky. Unfortunately, our belief that this is true will dissuade us from exploring how we might create a career we love.

In this way, we perpetuate the belief that we are controlled by our environment. We are limiting our career possibilities by the expectations and by what the majority considers possible. This belief is generally stronger in collective cultures where societal norms demand an individual's time and attention be spent in very scripted ways. For instance, some cultures uphold a traditional narrative that the father works while the mother stays home to take care of the children and household. The weight of expectations makes it harder for people to pursue their dreams and ambitions, enforcing the belief that their possibilities are limited.

As an example, in my culture of origin, the narrative was that a woman's role is only to have children and devote her time and efforts to the family. This cultural narrative made me believe I had to put my life on hold once I married. It took my first marriage going completely off the rails for me to put my career back at the forefront of my life. This was despite the fact that I had always been clear that I had no plans of giving up my studies or career. Yet, as soon as my ex-husband had to leave, his family immediately expected me to put my studies on hold. I cannot count the number of times my ex-father-in-law asked me why I wanted to finish my studies. He would always say, "Your husband makes more money than you know what to do with it. What's a degree going to give you that a husband cannot?" This coming from an educated man, a diplomat with a fiercely independent wife. My blessing was that my father always raised me with the belief that I had to always have the means for financial independence and the unspoken pressure to have a career that would give me status.

I have seen this belief limit many women from countries like Morocco, South Korea, Egypt, and India, especially women from privileged backgrounds. They have a strong desire to work after completing their studies, yet the culture's expectations of their roles as mothers and wives keep them catering to the demands of the family and unable to live their own dreams. And their privilege is used to invalidate their desire to work, as if money is the only reason to work.

It was eye-opening for me to see the same belief that women have to be the primary caregivers in families stopping western women from having a career they love. Though the consequences of the belief are different, it remains the same belief.

In western countries, it keeps women stuck in a cycle of chronic exhaustion, trying to navigate the demands of a family with work. However, as they are usually earning to supplement the family's income or are even primary earners, they will not give themselves permission to explore earning from their passions and gifts as they are too entrenched in the fear of not making sufficient income or failing in their role.

The Freedom of Choice

As a result, they often give up their well-being, empathy, and care to fit into the predominant model of working. Generally, the ability to pursue one's dream is secondary to the pursuit of status. If the dream does not adhere to the prevailing narrative that wealth and status are superior, one may never find the courage to pursue it.

> *But what if work was not meant to be for survival only? Perhaps our cultural narratives about the very nature and function of work in our lives are something to be examined?*

The example I shared above contrasts the belief about the role of women in individual and collective cultures. In cross-cultural training, we generally refer to individualistic cultures as those where the emphasis is on the individual responsibility for one's life, where the individual is encouraged from a young age to value their freedoms. Collective cultures are generally those where the family and community structures are more important than the individual. The individual is expected to take care of other members of the family, at times, even extended family. As they put the well-being of the community ahead of the individual, they receive care, nurturing, and often financial stability from others in return. In both individual and collective cultures, the individual wanting to create a career they love will think it is not possible, and that their culture does not allow it. For the man, financial obligations come first; and for the woman, the pursuit of personal accomplishments must come second, if at all, to family obligations.

In both cases, culture shapes the belief that work is meant to be for survival, rather than the joyful expression of one's talents and abilities; and these cultural narratives dictate beliefs, choices, and actions or inactions.

Regardless of their culture, the majority of people operate from the belief that others do things to them. This is perhaps most evident in language. When we have a conflict with someone and we say they have hurt us, the implication is that they hold power over our emotional state. Yet the action of this individual or the words they spoke to us could impact someone else very differently. In fact, what triggers pain for one person can leave another completely unaffected.

> We then face the realization that the emotion lives in us, the receiver, and that the speaker is the trigger and not the source.

Although the speaker triggered the emotion, they do not control our reaction to it. We retain the ability to own our reactions and emotions.

In the example of desiring a shift to a more meaningful career, the limiting belief is "I cannot have a meaningful career and make enough money." The logical and cultural beliefs might be "I cannot make the same income, and therefore will be a bad spouse, parent, etc...." or "I will be seen as a failure." Though we may be upset when we hear these statements, we may find ourselves suppressing our emotions, and therefore our dreams. We might feel misunderstood and alone, and therefore, give up on our dream. By adopting the limiting belief as true, we feel like a victim of our culture, our friends, or our employer, and give ourselves permission to stay in non-action, perpetuating the cycle of disempowerment.

When we cede control over our actions to others, we are subconsciously shifting the responsibility for our actions to them. Our internal dialogue is so embedded in our subconscious that we tie our ability to react differently to their behavior. Our thought process says others need to change, so we can be happy.

> *The disempowering belief that our well-being or happiness is reliant on our environment, our relationships, or other external factors gives us an out.*
>
> *It allows us to resist operating in our best interest by making our peace of mind dependent on the behavior of others.*

This is exactly what keeps us in the victim mindset. Only by letting go of this flawed reasoning can we start to act in our own interests.

Each of the three personas from the drama triangle has its own default ways of seeing the world, accompanied by a pattern of emotions, beliefs, and reactions that translate into the fight, flight, freeze, appease, or dissociate responses as coping mechanisms. Until we begin the introspection, we remain in this recurring pattern. How does one then step outside of the belief that we are at the mercy of other people's actions or limited by the beliefs and mindset we inherited? How can one reclaim a sense of agency?

> When we see life through the lens of what we cannot do because others do not allow it, we are living from a victim's mindset.

And our reaction will often be to blame others, or our culture for the choices we are not able to make. We find ourselves feeling sadness, confusion, and helplessness.

The reality is that more often than not, the action we would like to take is possible; however, we may not be able to recognize what that right action is, or we might be unwilling to pay the price it requires of us. This is the shift I experienced after my time off from work. I could no longer un-see that the cultural narrative that work was only for money and status was flawed. I had experienced illness and disillusionment by believing this narrative, and I had questioned what the real purpose of work was in my life beyond income.

According to Karpman's Drama Triangle, I wanted to stop playing the unconscious roles of victim, persecutor, and rescuer and start living in the empowered self, challenger/upstander, and coach roles.[16]

The Freedom of Choice

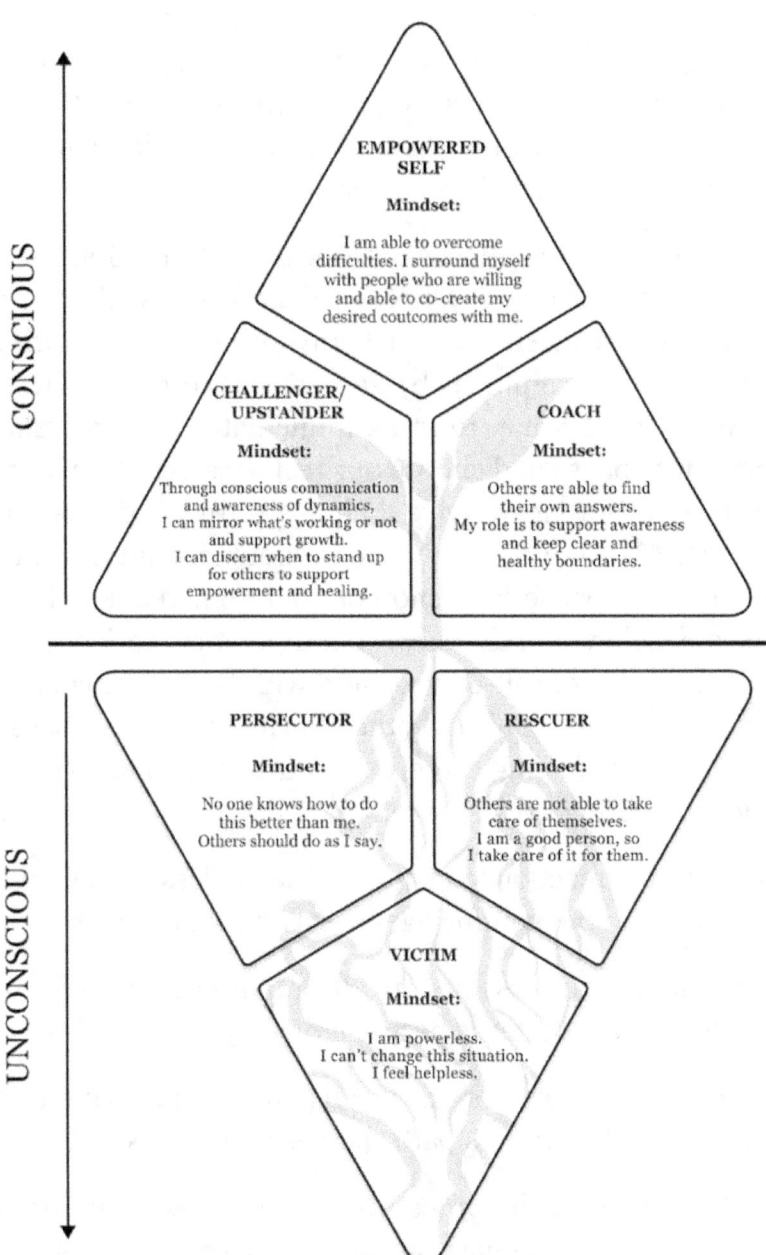

To take charge of one's life, a paradigm shift needs to occur: A recognition that disempowering beliefs trigger fear in us, and that although others might stimulate our emotions or have similar limiting beliefs, we still have a choice in how we respond and which beliefs we feed.

To do that, we need to acknowledge that emotions are a natural part of our psychological make-up while giving ourselves permission to feel any number of emotions when we are stimulated by someone's words or actions. However, rather than reacting immediately, we can take a moment to pause and choose our response. At first, we may not recognize that we have a choice to respond—we have been reacting automatically over a lifetime—and it will feel unnatural to pause for a moment before making a choice. Like any behavioral change, it takes practice, patience, and a healthy dose of self-compassion with the learning curve. The process is the same whether we are working on setting boundaries, changing careers, improving our management style, or creating world peace.

Moving from reaction to response, the process of reclaiming your power and regaining agency has three steps:

First, build awareness of your disempowering beliefs, and your behavioral patterns perpetuating them.

Second, make a conscious decision to respond with intention rather than react from a patterned behavior or belief.

And third, practice this process repeatedly to recondition your behavior from immediate reaction to measured response.

Trigger to Action

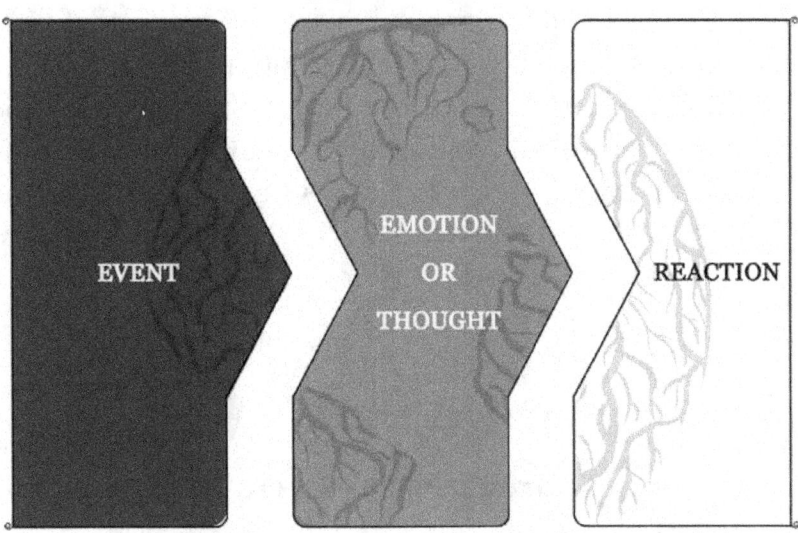

Once you begin to internalize this process and recognize your emotions, you will meet your inner critic and shadow. The shadow is the unconscious and stores fears, limiting beliefs, and traumas from unprocessed experiences. It is the source of your reaction. It is this shadow that we project onto others. As its name suggests, the shadow can be rather dark and dense, which is why most people spend their lives avoiding it. And with that, tragically, they lose out on the sense of empowerment that comes from befriending one's shadow.

There are numerous modalities and methodologies to connect with and transform the energy stored in the shadow. While the shadow can be referred to as a whole, I found in my practice that familiarizing yourself with your patterns becomes easier when you connect with parts of you that get activated as a result of emotions. Some parts are universal, like the inner critic; others are personal to you and your journey.

Whether you call it shadow, inner child, pain body, or any other name, the important thing is to recognize that your reactions are shaped by thoughts, emotions, and memories beyond your rational mind. You need to find the best tools that allow you to heal and restore balance and harmony, reconnecting you with your inner power.

Breaking the Cycle

My client had reached a point where she recognized that her long and great career was no longer fulfilling for her. On one hand, she felt an intense desire to take up different work. On the other hand, recurring thoughts that she was "too close to retirement age and would have too much to learn to start something new" kept her from exploring other career options. She was also worried about being perceived as flighty and stupid for changing careers because of the culture in which she was living. The potential loss of social status and financial stability were too great for her to risk. Yet, the desire to do meaningful work and leave a legacy for future generations persisted. There was a part of her longing for a different future and a part of her believing it was out of reach–and too scary to try.

We worked together to explore the real fears that were holding her back and to create clarity on the legacy she wanted to leave behind. We brought the conflict between her parts into harmony. This internal harmony allowed her

The Freedom of Choice

to see the deeper impact she longed to have and how she had already been doing it unconsciously throughout her career. Her perspective of the gap between her longing and her reality began to diminish, and her dream became more within reach. Her growing clarity on the essence of the impact she was seeking countered her limiting belief that she would have too much to learn and allowed her to acknowledge all the assets and skills she could capitalize on to make a shift. She gave herself permission to pursue initiatives towards the specific impact she wanted to have in working with women and youth through her existing career and aligned volunteer activities.

As our work progressed, she connected with the depth of sadness and unhappiness caused by focusing her time and energy on work that was not fulfilling her soul. She found the courage and determination to take the risk of starting over. This was a direct result of inner child healing sessions we had. Her perspective shifted from "I will lose status" to "Status is nice yet does not truly fulfill me or take away my sadness." We also addressed her fears about financial stability. She realized she had enough to be well; and when she looked more closely at her finances, she didn't need as much money as she initially thought. Today, this client is a thriving coach and advocate for women and youth.

Our coaching journey shifted her away from the limiting beliefs that she would lose social status and respect if she made a career shift. She went from a belief that her culture causes her to stay in her career to a belief that the dominant narrative in her culture is to only have one career throughout one's life, and yet that did not work for her. She also shifted from "I cannot make enough money as a coach" to "I have enough for me and my family's needs" and "I can create a thriving career as a coach as I grow my expertise." She moved from inaction to action around her dreams.

When people in her environment reacted to her initial career shift, they advised her to stay in her position for the same reasons: fear of losing status and concerns about her income. At first, her response wavered between trying to convince them that it was possible and being upset with them. Deep down, it triggered fear and self-doubt. Today, she recognizes they were simply coming from the dominant narrative within her culture, one in which she did not have the freedom to choose. With this perspective, she no longer reacts to them in a way that blames them or blames herself internally.

This is the journey of moving from reaction to response.

It allows us to recognize that we are not the product of other people's expectations, but the product of our choices.

This understanding gives us the freedom and wisdom to make our own choices and surround ourselves with people who are willing and able to grow with us. The part of my client that was angry at other people for advising her to stay within her career was, in fact, covering up her own fear and self-doubt. This is a part of the shadow.

As we face our shadow, we transform our hidden fear and emotional pain into productive energy that fuels our dreams instead of our fears. With that shift, we change our awareness of ourselves and start to navigate our inner landscape with clarity, wisdom, and authenticity. In this way, we are able to act on our dream, whether that is healing ourselves, getting a promotion, or transforming our world.

The Freedom of Choice

Our shadow usually holds a story, a narrative, and a perspective that is fear-based in order to protect us from perceived threats. Instead of being limited by these narratives and feeling powerless to create a life that is meaningful, we can teach ourselves to hear the story, and create a new and more empowering one. Brené Brown refers to this as the stories we tell ourselves in her interview with Oprah Winfrey.[17]

> When our beliefs about what we can or cannot do with our life go unchecked, unacknowledged, and unexplored, we are giving our power away in every interaction.

We go around blaming others and ourselves for the pain we feel, and we take away our ability to heal ourselves. We are effectively putting our emotional wellness in others' hands. To break the cycle, we need to take more time between intake and response. Without that pause, our immediate reaction is likely to escalate to inner and outer conflict, and inaction.

> *PRINCIPLE #3*
> We take all our actions, even the unconscious (re) actions as an attempt to meet a need.

Practice: Shifting Your Disempowering Stories

Actively making the decision to monitor your internal monologue and choosing how you respond helps you overcome the belief that you are powerless. Through small shifts in your responses, you can recapture inner power and change your outcomes.

1—Build awareness of your limiting beliefs.

Using a journal, make a list of 3 things you would really like to achieve and that would make you feel happier, healthier, and more empowered. Then, answer the question: "Why am I not taking action?" This will bring up some of your unconscious beliefs and assumptions.

2—Strengthen your inner witness and interrupt disempowering patterns.

I suggest you go through the next few days observing yourself and imagining you have a remote control. When you sense the intensity of any emotion getting too high, press pause. There is always a moment before you react, when you can actively interrupt the pattern. As soon as your inner witness becomes strong enough to catch that moment, you can imagine that you are pressing pause instead of automatically reacting.

1. Use your remote to pause. Take this moment to check your internal state and name your emotions.
2. Understand the story you are telling yourself. The story will be a source of unfulfilled expectations and unspoken assumptions. This internal narrative has three parts:
   - the story you tell yourself

- how the experience makes you feel
- the unmet needs it evokes

3. Once you understand yourself in the context of this experience, gauge alternatives to your interpretation. In the example I shared above, my client wanted a more meaningful career and began to move into action once she shifted her disempowering stories. Her belief went from "It would be too hard to make a shift to something new" to "I already have a solid base of skills and experience to build my new career," and from "I would lose status" to realizing the status she wanted to keep was, in fact, causing her suffering, rather than giving her the meaning and joy she was longing for.

When I began this practice, I used to share with my husband that I was triggered and was unclear why. I would withdraw and take time to name my feelings, needs, and stories before coming back to our conversation.

Others may not understand at the beginning. With time, they will begin to see the wisdom in your retreat, because you will come back with clarity, humility, and the ability to find mutually beneficial solutions.

Small Pauses Catalyze Better Choices

It took many pauses and reframes for me to reclaim my freedom in moments where I had previously given my power away to others, but consistent practice prepared me for that conversation with my manager about my *choice* to leave on my own terms.

Of course, I knew that the only thing I had control over in that moment was my own response, and I was worried about her reaction. Yet something amazing happened.

To my surprise, that conversation changed something. I soon found her willing to listen to what I thought was best for me and work with me to create win-wins. She called me a couple of days later and said she was willing to listen differently.

In taking responsibility for my needs, advocating unapologetically for myself, and putting my well-being first, I had owned my truth and was able to take the next steps needed to change the outcome. Our conversations from that point on became a lot more open and vulnerable. She even shared details of their own struggle; and indirectly, I learned how the unspoken rules of staying silent in the face of intimidation and toxicity were upheld at different levels. It was the very pattern I was there to change for myself.

"If you focus on results, you will never change. If you focus on change, you will get the results."
~Jack Dickson~

CHAPTER 4

The Reclamation of Inner Power

I've done it!

In my heart, sadness competed with elation. Sadness that we create such dehumanizing workplaces. And elation that I had now survived and grown from the experience.

Standing outside, I looked at the building that had been the scene of my psychological descent into hell and took stock of the "return to work" experience. I recalled the first day I had walked in through those glass doors, filled with hope, proud to serve my country. Glancing down the narrow street, I looked at the surrounding buildings and the empty lot my colleagues and I crossed to go to the drugstore on our lunch breaks. It all felt familiar and foreign at the same time. Stepping off the sidewalk, I got into my car.

I am not the same person I was when I walked in there six months ago. I stopped giving my power away and owned it.

This was my moment of reclamation. Not only had I managed to go back to work, I now knew with certainty I wasn't the problem. I had faced my worst fear and closed the door on a damaging pattern. Memories of courageous choices to advocate for myself in the face of dehumanizing adversity floated through my mind as I prepared to leave that parking lot for the last time. Courageous, tough conversations with higher-ups and peers and holding my ground about reducing my hours so I could work with another organization were victories I was proud to walk away with today.

I stared at the building in my rear-view mirror, surprised to feel gratitude warming my chest—gratitude that I was finally setting myself free of the pain.

Well done, Kawtar, I said to myself. *It wasn't easy, but you did it. I am proud of you.*

With a deep sense of completion, I turned my eyes back to the road and drove home. It was time to open a new chapter in my professional life.

> ### DISEMPOWERING BELIEF #4
> We can buy happiness.

The truth was that I had been on the journey of reclaiming my power for a few years by the time I finished law school, found myself in this toxic environment, opted to go on sick leave, and then walked back into that building determined to take the next big steps to my freedom.

A large part of my healing process emerged from my decision to work in a different environment. My confidence had been so shaken by the intimidation and my health crisis, my therapist and I were both wondering what I was truly capable of professionally. The only way to find out was to work in a job that was more aligned with my values and offered a better environment. Just as this realization set in, I received an opportunity to work in a community organization, supporting low-income families and advocating for their needs.

For a few months, I juggled two jobs with the intention of healing. Working in two radically different environments where initiative, communication, teamwork, and support were applied in opposite ways actually helped me resolve much of the dissonance I had been carrying—a dissonance we are conditioned into.

In today's age, we live in societies that constantly solicit us to consume. Goods, services, and information are available in greater abundance than ever before, and media and advertising industries are built on consumption. Credit is always available and easy to access, despite the fact that too much credit impoverishes. Through television, we consume news and other stories, often in an attempt to numb the hole we feel growing within, but even that practice reinforces the message to consume more with its constant advertising.

The result of this modus operandi of consumption is that most people embark on a merry-go-round life. Going to a job they dislike, which makes them unhappy, anxious, and exhausted. Going home to consume food, drink, and information to numb the pain, only to be targeted by cleverly created advertising that studies their behavior to encourage greater consumption. Waking up the next day to continue the cycle. This disempowering dynamic is debilitating to the human spirit. It's like you leave the shore to sail into the horizon after graduation or when you begin working, believing you are equipped for your dreams and a successful and happy life. Then, as you slowly lose sight of the horizon, you find yourself unable to re-route. Most people around you live in the same cycle, so it seems normal. However, is this perspective of what is normal truly healthy or productive?

I remember the merry-go-round all too well. Working, trapped behind a large gray cubicle or, later, in a nice office, still feeling stuck. Deep down, I knew something was off. I knew the anxiety attacks couldn't be normal. I knew that long-term medication was not the answer, yet it was what most people did. I intuitively knew I didn't have to, and wouldn't, be a victim of the cycle forever. But how was I going to turn the tide? I was about to get an education into the myriad ways we learn to give our power away.

When the soul is exhausted, it becomes easy to numb the increasing pain with even more consumption. We think we need that next car, promotion or relationship, that newer gadget or bigger television set. We do this under the assumption that when we have it, all will be better, and our internal discomfort and pain will magically disappear. But do they?

One way we perpetuate this vicious cycle is with our misunderstanding of the word *need*. Today, the words *need* and *want* are used interchangeably. Yet if we look at their formal definitions, there is a significant difference between *needing* something and *wanting* something. According to Merriam-Webster's Dictionary, a *need* is a physiological or psychological requirement for the well-being of an organism while a *want* is something for which we have a strong desire.

While *wants* can vary between individuals, *needs* are fairly consistent. Human needs are well-documented by Professor

Abraham Maslow and illustrated by the following diagram of the hierarchy of needs.[18] These needs, ranging from the physiological to the psychological, are universal for well-being. *Wants*, on the other hand, can be physical (a car, house, etc.) or abstract (love, power, or influence).

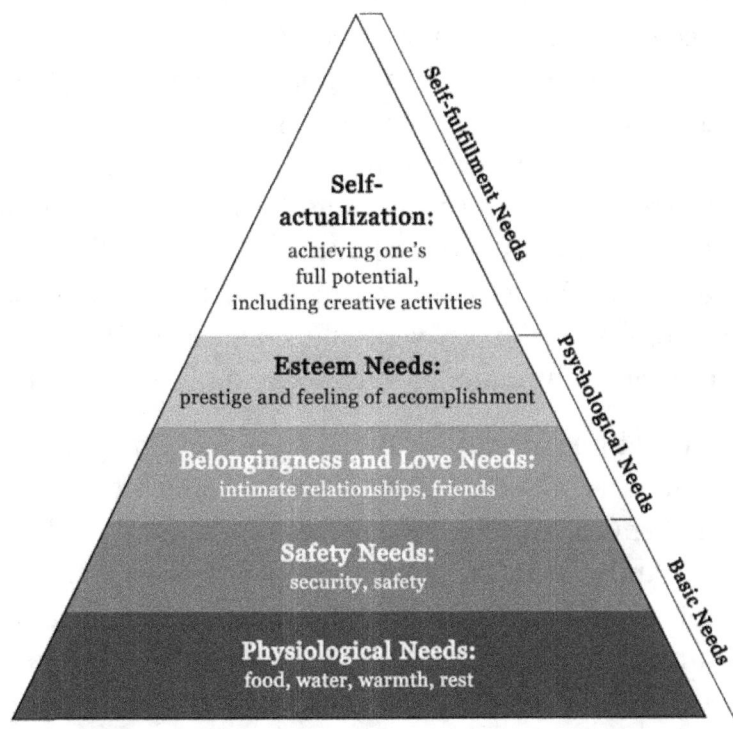

Notice that there is an overlap between *needs* and *wants*. Human beings start from a place of need; sustenance, shelter, clothing, love, support, and friendship are all critical needs for well-being.

The difference between a *need* and a *want* is subtle. How often have you seen something and said, "I want that," or "I need that"? At their essence, needs are something that, once met, give us a sense of fulfillment. When we satiate a *need*, we feel content, satisfied, or even grateful. When we attain a *want*, on the other hand, it is usually not as fulfilling as expected.

A *want* is something we thought was a need, but it really wasn't. The sense of contentment from having a *want* attained is usually very short-lived. Rather than engendering a deep sense of contentment, *wants* keep us striving for the next big thing—a new purchase, a new job, a new relationship—in order to attain the sense of satisfaction we crave. This perpetuates the conditioning that happiness hinges on the possession of something more than what we have now. Rather than getting us closer to the sense of satisfaction we long for, we remain locked in the cycle of consumption, numbing the deeper discomfort driving it.

A good example of this is a 1978 psychology study in which researchers from Northwestern University and the University of Massachusetts compared the happiness levels of lottery winners and victims of catastrophic accidents.[19] They found that lottery winners, once they have internalized the thrill of winning and splurged on their *wants*, were generally less happy than victims of accidents. The researchers found that a year after the payout, the lottery winners reverted to the same level of happiness (or unhappiness) that they had before they won. Some were even worse off due to relationship changes caused by the lottery win.

"Eventually, the thrill of winning the lottery will itself wear off... Thus, as lottery winners become accustomed to the additional pleasures made possible by their new wealth, these pleasures should be experienced as less intense and

The Reclamation of Inner Power

should no longer contribute very much to their general level of happiness."[20]

In essence, lottery winners' newfound wealth became commonplace, and they needed to consume even more to achieve the same level of happiness they felt after winning. They became stuck in a cycle of wanting more and more to regain their post-lottery "happiness," leaving them even further from true happiness. So if acquiring more is not the answer, how do we break the cycle and find fulfillment?

Maslow's hierarchy of *needs* shows that once physical needs are met, it's time to tend to psychological and self-actualization needs. Unfortunately, the culture of striving gives us the illusion that our physical needs are never really met; and even when we feel they are, we have no idea how to fulfill our psychological and self-actualization needs. Our cultures do not yet offer us the language and tools to fulfill these needs. To make matters worse, attempts to fulfill these needs with tools like therapy, coaching, and contemplative practices can be seen as shameful. Yet, it is within these practices that we find the answer.

Considering that we all have unprocessed emotional experiences, does it make any sense to feel shame when seeking tools to help us process experiences and become emotionally competent and content? Are we to live our entire lives braving through our early wounds to prove that we are strong? The truth is genuine strength can only be achieved and sustained through processing our disempowering patterns, which puts us back in our power.

One need we all have as humans is the need for power. Not power *over* others, but rather power *within* our own lives.

We seek a real sense of agency and the ability to shape our own paths, rather than being shaped by the influences of events, situations, and people. The feelings of powerlessness and helplessness underlying our inability to shape our own lives is the greatest source of frustration, anger, and fear that we carry in our hearts and bodies. It is also the source of all conflicts.

In one of my workshops, I taught techniques for deep listening along with strategies for how to articulate feelings. When we used the techniques to tackle conflict towards the end of the session, one member of the leadership team deeply reflected, "So Kawtar, it looks like in essence, all conflicts are a struggle for power."

When we recognize this truth, we reconnect with an immense amount of inner power. We strengthen our ability to address our core needs, and we stop desperately seeking to satisfy whimsical wants. We reconnect with our inner power to shape outcomes, and therefore our lives. We seek out mutually beneficial solutions. This inner power is available to all of us regardless of the culture, age, profession, or gender we identify with. Though dominant groups have easier access to it. We do a disservice to everyone if we perpetuate the false belief that we have equal access to our inner power. Due to factors such as generational trauma and systemic inequities, marginalized groups have more internal and external barriers. And this is further nuanced by the complex intersectionalities of our identities. However, the possibility of reclaiming that inner power, even in the context of systemic inequities, exists. The question is whether we will reclaim it.

The Reclamation of Inner Power

Take a moment to look at the list of *needs* below and see how you feel when you read these words. I find in my coaching and consulting practice that whenever clients connect with their authentic needs, their experience of life changes. They gain ease, a sense of clarity, and empowerment. Surprisingly, their consumption habits change as well. One of my coaching teachers and author, Martha Lasley, defines power as "the ability to meet needs."

Once we connect with this power and cultivate trust in our ability to meet our own needs, the numbing of consumption is no longer required.

While most people go through life uneducated about their real needs, trying desperately to meet psychological needs with physical objects and status symbols, the internal and external conflicts grow. This is further reinforced in the media with the crux of advertising being less to inform than persuade. At a deeper level though, feelings of satisfaction, happiness, and contentment truly come from having *needs*, rather than *wants*, met.

Marshall Rosenberg, founder of The Center for Non-Violent Communication, created an inventory of universal human needs that is an invaluable resource for the journey of unfolding peace.[21]

Needs[22]

PHYSICAL

Shelter
Air
Food
Movement/Exercise
Safety
Water
Touch
Rest
Sexual Expression

INTERDEPENDENCE

Acceptance
Appreciation
Closeness
Consideration
Community
Contribution
Emotional Safety
Empathy
Honesty

INTEGRITY

Authenticity
Creativity
Meaning
Self-worth

AUTONOMY

To choose one's dreams, goals, values
To choose one's plan for fulfilling those
Of dreams fulfilled
Of loss (mourning)

SPIRITUAL COMMUNION

Beauty
Harmony
Peace
Order
Inspiration
Play
Fun
Laughter

Celebration of Life
Love
Respect
Reassurance
Support
Trust
Understanding
Warmth

The Reclamation of Inner Power

Breaking The Cycle

Below are some examples of unmet needs I regularly encounter with clients in my coaching and consulting practice. The scenarios below are linked to conflict because suppressing unmet needs creates internal conflict, which often translates into external conflict.

Example 1: Inner Conflicts Due to Unmet Needs

When exploring with clients who feel dissatisfied with their careers, cultural programming often comes up as a barrier. These clients often start their exploration at a breaking point when their health has declined or when they can no longer live with their intense feelings of dissatisfaction. By this point, their self-esteem and confidence have weakened. They are constantly confronted by negative messaging in subtle and not-so-subtle ways with questions like, "How will you make money if you start over? You will lose everyone's respect and trust," and messages such as, "It's risky, who are you to make such a drastic change?" or "Everyone just tries to get by. How can you imagine you can change things?"

At this stage, their unmet needs for meaning, self-worth, creativity, and contribution are screaming to be met. Clients end up existing between these two spaces, where their needs for self-determination and contribution feel at odds with their needs for respect, safety, and acceptance. Like me early in my journey, they cannot silence the inner nudge to take a risk and do what calls them, as irrational as it seems.

I have come to recognize there is an evolutionary explanation for this phenomenon. Some of us are wired differently and have a higher need for self-expression, meaning, and contribution—so high, in fact, that those individuals face difficulty fitting in, which then shakes their confidence. If you fall into this dynamic, I'd like to offer you Einstein's wise words: "Everybody is a genius. But if you judge a fish by its ability to climb a tree, it will live its whole life believing it is stupid." Many clients have reshaped their careers, taking brave and rewarding steps in new and initially scary directions. Know that you are not alone, and there are many ways to step outside of this cycle. You can hear more about how I made my career shift in this interview.[23]

Example 2: Family Conflict Due to Unmet Needs

While leading a group coaching session, one woman realized the extent to which living abroad for her husband's job was causing her sadness and near desperation. Unable to obtain a permit for work, her needs for meaning, creativity, authenticity, appreciation, and autonomy remained unmet. This made her resent living abroad and created latent tension in her marriage, which often showed up in arguments about raising the kids, household chores, and even weekend activities.

From her perspective, she was shouldering the entire responsibility for the household and not being appreciated for her contribution. She was also deeply concerned about sharing this with her husband for fear of creating conflict.

The Reclamation of Inner Power

Ironically, not sharing her feelings was causing just as much tension and conflict. Upon deeper inquiry, she identified her real unmet needs and reflected on strategies to meet them. She saw that her dominant strategies up to that point were avoidance of the topic and the company of her husband altogether, hints to her husband with the hopes that he would sense what she was going through, or being upset but denying to herself and her husband the reasons why. None of these strategies were creating connection or intimacy in her family life or resolving her unmet needs. Her frustration only grew. Knowing this dynamic is one of the main reasons why couples living internationally have one of the higher divorce rates, she wanted to create a different outcome in her story.

With some guidance and communication strategies, she was able to share her truth with her husband. To her surprise, he was not defensive. Instead, he understood what she was going through. Together they devised a plan for her to ensure she keeps a professional thread alive in her life despite the challenges of global living. They even made sure she had self-care time when he took care of the kids. A few months later, he reported to her how much closer he felt to his children and how happy he was to have that time with them. By breaking down the larger picture, they were able to find ways for both their needs to be met, while continuing their global lifestyle—which was important to both of them.

Example 3: Workplace Conflict Due to Unmet Needs

A few years ago, I was collaborating on a project with a colleague. I prepared my part, then sent it to my colleague to add hers so we could finalize and share it with our manager. As the deadline approached, I had not yet heard back from her and was getting concerned about missing the deadline–something I really dislike. At the time, I had been practicing naming my emotions and identifying my needs. I looked at my list and realized that underlying my feelings of annoyance and upset were my needs for trust, support, and respect. I understood that what was upsetting to me was not so much that she might not do her part, but rather that she was silent. I did not want to interpret her silence inaccurately, by either giving her the benefit of the doubt and then receiving an unpleasant surprise, or assuming she did not want to do the work and add to my workload unnecessarily. I decided to call and ask about the status of the work.

Taking a clear approach as to what was important for me in that situation, I was able to be calm, present, and empathetic. During our conversation, I noticed her tone change and I felt something was off. I shared this observation with her, noting that I was in no way intending to create a blame game and that my sole concern was missing the deadline. Suddenly, my colleague opened up to me about her health challenges. Together, we came to an informal agreement that I would take on additional work to allow her time for recovery, while she would keep me posted on her recovery and gradually take on more work over the following weeks. I felt reassured that we would still deliver on time and comfortably because we had created an accountability structure.

By the deadline, the project was ready for submission and deemed a success. In addition, my colleague had fully recovered and was able to take on more work in the next round. With mutual vulnerability, authenticity, and care, we were able to address the situation, meet our needs, and prevent potential conflicts along the way.

We both had high needs for contribution, understanding, and care; and our mutual acknowledgment of this turned us from colleagues to friends. However, it is important to recognize that when faced with someone with a high need for control and power (i.e. a persecutor profile from the Empowerment Triangle), this strategy is not the best suited because such a person usually uses blame strategies and force, rather than empathy, authenticity, and transparency. This power dynamic requires presence and discernment to act appropriately in the moment.

> *PRINCIPLE #4*
> *Differentiating needs from wants aligns us with our inner power.*

Practice: Identifying Needs

1–Identify the Real Need
When you find yourself thinking you need something, pause and review the Universal Needs list. What is the core need you are trying to meet?

2–Reclaim Your Inner Power
When you find yourself upset by a situation, go back to the lists of feelings, followed by the list of needs. Focus on naming your emotions, and then differentiating between your needs and wants.

Once you name your core need, identify the strategy (action or inaction) you are using to meet your need.

Brainstorm 3 ways that you can meet this need differently.

We will take these explorations deeper as we move through the coming chapters.

Reconciling and Reclaiming is a Practice

The contrast of the two starkly different work environments made it so easy to see how one enhanced my sense of personal power and the other chipped away at it. One had a motivated and smiling team; the other touted a record number of employees on sick leave. One had leaders who empowered employees to use all of their skills and took responsibility for their failures; the other operated from an abusive power dynamic.

In other words, it finally hit home. I wasn't the problem. I was *never* the problem. The problem was the dynamic happening "out there" that I *consented to* because I was too scared of being labeled as difficult, or incompetent and being excluded. At the time, I was not yet able to articulate what was happening or recognize the toxic leadership dynamic—a common issue for victims of abuse. I could feel something was off; but until my mind was able to make sense of it through therapy, I was stuck in feeling and believing that I was powerless. The retraumatization threw me back into the disbelief and confusion that victims of abuse struggle with, especially in the face of gaslighting. And in my case, this was not only personal but systemic. I could not believe that this dynamic was so intense in Canada, and the disbelief took time to wear off.

The Reclamation of Inner Power

It was such a disconnect from the Canada I knew and experienced before. And yet here it was: this, too, was Canada. It was the place in which I had spent my teenage years waiting to live freely and supposedly, as an equal under the law and the place in which I had sought refuge after leaving the abusive dynamic with my first husband. I know it sounds naive but, on an unconscious level, being the child of immigrants meant that I was coming to a place where the economics and social dynamics were better. But it turns out, all human dynamics are universal. And the dynamics of violence, intimidation, and abuse are everywhere. So are the dynamics of denial, and pretending we are perfect, instead of owning our imperfections. It's always easier to look out there, at other people and countries, and condemn their ways. How could Canada, the place where I received support and resources to put my life back together, escape the past, and start afresh, be the same place where this ugliness exists? How could I, after all I had gone through, be seen as a potential threat? How could they not see how much I love this place? How could anyone justify that my security clearance was stalled with my profile? It made no sense. It took some time to make peace with this and hold both love and gratitude with the sadness, disillusionment, and anger. Ultimately, it was empowering to see that I do not have to be a passive consumer of this culture. I could now become an active participant and engaged citizen in shaping a country where we live our values more fully.

Within six months, as I kept investing time and energy in my community work, I was enjoying the reward of seeing the families speaking with elected leaders, sharing their struggles, and getting decisions reversed. In that environment, I brought together all the communication and self-empowerment tools I had learned so far to support these families, which confirmed for me that I was on the right path. I now knew that working in alignment with my values in an environment where I had trust, freedom to use my skills and creativity, and a supportive team, I could thrive. Even the anxiety had reduced despite everyone's concern.

I could have listened to those who said that leaving a secure government position was career suicide. I could have limited myself with other people's fears and opinions. But I knew that path was not mine. However, making peace with this loss was a long process. I grieved the loss of the income, the loss of security, the unfulfilled dreams, the institutional disillusionment, and a future serving the country I had chosen to call home for a long time.

"Peace is not the absence of conflict, it is the ability to handle conflict by peaceful means."
~Ronald Reagan~

CHAPTER 5

The Empowerment of Meeting Needs

As I walked toward the boardroom with a new client, I took in as much information as I could. He looked to be in his forties and presented himself nonchalantly, even though his expression and movements communicated distress.

"I've been through this before, so I know the drill…" he started and continued to tell us his story—multiple marriages and families, bitter endings, and alimony payments he could not afford. He was the victim, forced to pay for the sustenance of the children he had fathered when everything was their mothers' fault.

As we sat down at the conference table, I looked out the big window to collect myself.

He seems really convinced that he played no role in these situations. Does he not recognize that he made these children? How could he think he is a victim for having to provide for them? Not once, or twice, but three times.

Turning back toward him, I saw a man in denial, stuck in a pattern.

Ugh. I was so frustrated, thinking that this man needed so much more than just legal support. I couldn't help but think of the pain this trail of children he leaves behind must be suffering. He needed someone to help him see and shift this pattern of thinking and behavior that was creating so much pain.

Being trained as a lawyer, yet seeing a festering two-year conflict find resolution through a few conversations in mediation had recently flipped my professional world upside-down.

Why are we spending so many resources on these legal resolutions, clogging up the system, exacerbating stress for people, and paying incredible amounts of money when getting people to speak to each other with the right tools could bring resolution faster, at a lesser emotional, physical, and financial cost? Of course, there were many cases that would still require legal resolution. *But why is that the norm instead of the exception?* I wondered. *How could we make real solutions available to more people?*

These were the questions I asked myself as I focused on rebuilding my career. But I was at an impasse. Despite having loved my legal studies, I was not sure I could work as a lawyer. Something had changed in me; and I did not have words to articulate it, much less make sense of its implications for my career. If I were to articulate it today, I'd say that my values of empowerment, harmony, and justice had been crushed during those years at my previous workplace; and I was looking for a way to work in alignment with those values again.

At that moment, all I knew was that contribution was still a strong value for me; but I wondered if law was the vessel for my contribution. *Is it law that doesn't fit anymore, or is it law in the public sector?* I wondered. Once again, the

The Empowerment of Meeting Needs

answer would only be found in trying. I had called my best friend, a lawyer in private practice, and gone to spend a week job-shadowing her, doing everything private-sector lawyers do in their day-to-day. Sure enough, my answer was waiting there in that meeting with the gentleman who needed much more than what a lawyer could give him. I could see very clearly what the legal issues were, the research we'd have to do, and the answers we could provide. And yet everything in me wanted to talk about the human pattern at the heart of the problem. I could see it clear as day. And he seemed unable to see it. But that was not mine to point out.

What was mine to be concerned with was the realization that my work would have to contribute to people and help them solve their problems from the root causes, not just the symptoms.

> **DISEMPOWERING BELIEF #5**
> *Conflict is bad.*

Harmony is such an important human need that most individuals and cultures in the world encourage suppressing or hiding conflict.

For me, growing up in an Arab culture, the word conflict was seldom used. It is not that there was no conflict, as much as it was that conflict was taboo, completely ignored, and suppressed. The assumption was always that conflict leads to loss—loss of relationships, loss of respect, loss of money, loss of jobs. I spent the first thirty years of my life avoiding conflict at all costs without any cognitive awareness of my avoidance. It was simply an automatic response to maintain harmony because it was a topic that was never discussed. Conflict avoidance was actively encouraged, and as a woman especially, it was strongly advised.

Imagine my shock and surprise when I learned that assertiveness is, in fact, what protects a person from emotional assault.

The belief that conflict is bad and must be avoided is prevalent in cultures from Africa to Asia. Even in the West, where there is a slightly greater acceptance of disagreement and conflict, the ability to constructively manage it remains very low. While the avoidance of conflict can be justified by the fear of loss, the reality is that conflict avoidance has devastating effects on individuals, workplaces,[24] and the world.

Research shows that in the United States, bad bosses cost the economy between US$360 and US$500 billion annually in lost productivity, turnover, and higher health expenses. In Europe, research shows the cost of workplace stress ranges from US$220 million to US$187 billion in productivity loss and health care costs.[25]

At the organizational level, evidence shows conflict as being the cause of higher absenteeism, higher turnover, lower productivity, more frequent accidents and errors, lower profitability, and lower share price.[26] Put simply, employees too often leave jobs in order to get away from toxic bosses and escape conflict.

The Empowerment of Meeting Needs

Combining the belief that conflict is to be avoided with our lack of preparedness to constructively manage it, we become locked into conflict dynamics. When this occurs in the immediate family sphere or at work, it exposes us to chronic stress. Our health is affected adversely by the somatic indicators of the cost of conflict. What begins with emotional suffering turns into physical illness due to chronic stress. Too often, we choose to numb these symptoms with medication only rather than process and release the emotions behind them. When I began my healing journey, I was astonished to find that much of the stress that was locked in my body and deep tissue came from repressed emotions and traumatic memories.

At a personal level, stress, anxiety, heart disease, emotional distress, and depression, in addition to poor performance and relatively poorer quality work, are all hidden costs of conflict. Stress contributes to as much as 50% higher voluntary turnover in workplaces. At a global level, conflict, violence, and war were estimated to cost our economies $13.6 trillion in 2015.[27]

Though these numbers are staggering, the prevalence of conflict is not surprising when we consider that conflict is, at its core, an emotional experience, not a physical one. Therefore, addressing it at the physical level only allows it to be recreated repeatedly, sometimes in other areas of our lives.

In reality, conflict is the expression of unmet needs which trigger difficult emotions. No matter how much we try to externalize conflict, the reality remains that it is an internal, emotional experience. Countries do not feel. Wars are not started by machines.

Behind every conflict stand individuals, whether at the United Nations, in a boardroom in New York City, or in any home across the globe. The sooner we own this truth about ourselves, the faster we can take responsibility by making conflict transformation an integral part of our education systems, designing mandatory training programs, and creating more harmony in our world.

President Barack Obama refers to this in an interview for the Obama Foundation. In the interview, he speaks about finding the same dynamics at the level of community organizing, the State Senate, and G20 meetings with world leaders: "Same dynamics, it's just that there is a bigger spotlight, a bigger stage…the nature of human dynamics does not change from level to level."[28]

Perhaps the real issue behind our collective avoidance of conflicts is a lack of trust in our ability to resolve them constructively. If we associate conflict with loss, it is natural that the majority of us seek to avoid it.

This belief might be reinforced by the fact that on the opposite end of avoidant behavior toward conflict is the role of "persecutors" from the Empowerment Triangle. Persecutors are individuals with a high need for power, which they project externally. They demonstrate a strong belief that they have the answers and everyone should follow their lead. The reality, however, is that prosecutors typically have little ability to feel empathy and demonstrate a low level of emotional competence, hence a low ability to acknowledge their ignorance or mistakes. They are unable to regulate their emotional states and blame others for their actions, decisions, and reactions. Due to these characteristics, they dominate conversations and decision-making. As a result, societies have been traditionally driven by motivations of power, money, and success, creating a paradigm where most people feel alienated and powerless to assert their needs.

Breaking The Cycle

As much as this can be overwhelming when seen in the larger picture, the good news is that we all have the ability to rewire our patterned behavior in the face of conflict. We can develop the ability and strength to be comfortable with conflict while also holding conflicting needs with care.

As your perception and experience of conflict change, you will come to see that it is only the expression of opposing needs. When interpreted skillfully and with awareness, conflict provides information that transforms situations and changes breakdowns to breakthroughs.

Let's revisit some of the concepts from earlier chapters to see how the same methodology applies in conflict transformation at home, in the workplace, and even in tense situations such as war.

Conflict Transformation at Home

A client came into our session feeling exhausted and on the brink of tears. She'd had yet another argument with her husband. She wanted to spend time with him and the kids, yet it seemed like no matter how many times she told her husband this, he did not hear her. I asked her to describe how the conversation typically went. She noticed as she was speaking that it is a repeating cycle of events.

On weekends, her husband pursued his own interests and did not take care of the children. Spending little time as a couple or family, she felt alone despite the fact that they were all together. The times she tried to talk to him about it, he told her he didn't know what to do and the conversation would end there.

I asked her to name her emotions around the experience. She felt frustrated, irritated, worn out, worried, and underneath it all, sad. Tears started to roll as she felt the sadness. She realized how much she missed fun times together with her husband and the feeling of really being together. With this realization, her real needs slowly emerged: connection, warmth, understanding, and support.

As we continued our dissection, she realized that for her, it wasn't really about him taking care of specific tasks or failing to do something. What she really needed was connection, more than anything. It was the primary need she had to tend to. We discussed what makes her feel connected to her husband, what works for her, what works for him, and how she might be able to create more of that connection in their marriage. The next step was for her to share these insights in a vulnerable conversation with him, using the communication principles she had learned through our work.

By the end of our coaching engagement a few months later, the couple had created a new relationship and taken specific times to be together. They were more open about what created connection or disconnection for each of them and they felt closer to each other than they had in years. By learning to listen deeply to her feelings and needs, sharing her needs with her husband vulnerably, and taking time to articulate strategies, she was able to recreate the joy that had gone missing in her marriage and family life.

Conflict Transformation in Workspaces

We began our session with my client sharing a conflict occurring on a board on which she was serving. One individual was leading the board in a direction that she and others were concerned about, yet no one seemed able to stop it. We examined the assumptions being made and the disconnect she was experiencing between her gut instinct and her thoughts. She could feel something was off but did not have the words to articulate it. When we looked deeper, we discovered she was scared of saying something and being wrong or cast out for it, while her intuition was loudly telling her there was something unclear in this situation and that the words and actions of this individual were not aligned. Not wanting to cause trouble, she remained quiet.

When we explored what was at stake, she talked about the mandate of the organization not being respected and individuals losing their self-confidence and trust in each other. What used to be a harmonious atmosphere with transparent decision-making had become an unclear space with undertones and tension. The board had trusted this individual to take the entity to higher ground, yet the facts did not validate that he was living up to this trust. The thought of confronting this was overwhelming, yet the feeling of responsibility, the desire to be in integrity with her mandate, and the concern for the organization gave her the courage to acknowledge and confront the damaging impact of this person's behavior.

With her internal conflict resolved, she called a meeting to examine the situation more closely. Once the facts were looked at independent of emotion, the board members were able to identify their concerns, claim their need for collaboration, and create a way for accountability. A few weeks later, the decision-making was back on track, the accountability structures clear, and collaboration restored. The community's needs and mandate were again the primary focus of the board, rather than the time and effort spent on one individual's behavior.

What could have been a long, drawn-out process was prevented and turned around because of the courage of a leader to harness their inner power, deal with conflict, and transform a situation. Often, employees who care deeply for people and for ensuring integrity end up having to resign from organizations because they lack the internal and external resources and support to create and sustain a culture of accountability, transparency, and empowerment. This comes at a large financial and health cost to these organizations and our societies.

The Empowerment of Meeting Needs

Conflict Transformation in the World

For decades, Dr. Scilla Elworthy has worked toward creating a more peaceful world. She has supported peace negotiations and brought together parties in conflict at international levels to listen and discuss alternatives to war and nuclear arms. She is the co-founder of Peace Direct, author of *The Business Plan for Peace*, and a three-time Nobel Peace Prize Nominee. Dr. Elworthy shares the story of U.S. Lieutenant Colonel Chris Hughes, who was leading his men down the streets of Najaf, Iraq when the streets began to flood with people yelling and screaming. Instead of firing at them, Hughes instructed his men to kneel. The terrified soldiers followed his command, which led to complete silence for almost two minutes. Slowly, everyone started going back into their homes. Even in the context of war, deep presence and wisdom have been shown to prevent further bloodshed.[29]

> PRINCIPLE #5
> The higher purpose of conflict is to hold opposing needs with equal care.

Practice: From Awareness to Transformation

At this point, you have likely practiced naming your emotions and your core needs. When conflict arises, it is an indication that there are conflicting needs. This does not mean the conflicting needs are irreconcilable; it only means they are at odds in your current perspective of the situation.

When you name your need, your mind opens to different possibilities of how it can be met. As you practice identifying three options for the first while, you will increase your flexibility. This allows your brain to move from the usual binary pattern of polarity to learning to see the larger picture and expand the realm of possibilities. It connects you with your creative side and comes up with strategies that did not seem possible before this process. In the example above, with my client and her husband, her need was for connection. During our session, she realized that even when her husband was with her at home, her need for connection was still unmet. We closely examined what created the feeling of connection for her, and from there, created a strategy.

In her conversation with her husband, she asked him to double-check that her assumption about what creates connection for him was valid. From this clarity, they were able to create adapted strategies. They designed a way for each of them to take care of themselves separately, identified time they would share as a couple without kids, and agreed on activities with the kids. Together, they learned to cultivate a feeling of connection in everyday life.

When you are speaking with someone who is willing and able to articulate their emotions and needs, it makes the process much faster. However, even when you are dealing with someone who is not able to articulate their needs, you can make an educated guess as to what their unmet needs are and attempt to steer the conversation towards mutually satisfying strategies.

Over the next few days, notice how you deal with conflict. Do you run away from it, or do you get angry and fight back?

The Empowerment of Meeting Needs

Perhaps you just freeze and find yourself unable to think on your feet.

Be gentle with yourself as you explore. This conflict avoidance can be linked to traumatic memories and experiences. Remember that your survival patterns have been practiced unconsciously for a lifetime in your body and mind. It can take time to re-wire them.

Stage 1—For now, begin with building deeper awareness. Practice being present, noticing, naming emotions, and calming your brain with deep breathing when you feel triggered. In the next chapter, we will discuss the topic of self-care, which will make this process easier.

Stage 2—Once you become very aware of your reactionary pattern in conflict, I invite you to explore your internal triggers. What thoughts and emotions do you notice when you are in a conflict situation?

If the emotions triggered by this exercise get too strong, refer to the self-care chapter and create a self-care plan and, if needed, find a qualified professional for personalized support and guidance.

Meeting My Own Needs

It felt like I was creating an impossibly complex puzzle. I now had to find a career that would express my most important values, meet my needs for space to take care of my health, and be intellectually stimulating yet heart- and people-centered. Of course, it also had to provide an income that would be sufficient to guarantee my financial independence as a woman. So, back to research I went until I finally settled on mediation. That felt like a perfect career that combined my background, strengths, values, and aspirations. Or again, so I thought. A twist was just around the corner. But even then, this clarity gave me the strength needed to move through the coming obstacles.

"Support yourself with kind thoughts, loving words, and self-empowering acts."

~Iyanla Vanzant~

CHAPTER 6

The Holism of Self-Care

"Being immersed in so much that is unfamiliar will likely trigger anxiety, and emptiness may trigger depression." My therapist's words emerged from somewhere in the back of my mind to answer my unspoken questions. I sat in bed, watching the minutes and hours pass by, and felt paralyzed with fear. My stomach felt on fire, my breathing shallow. I could barely think.

What is happening? Could this, too, be just PTSD? I know it's fear, but it has never been this intense.

Before my departure for South Korea, she had warned me that anxiety might get triggered again. She was right. About six months into being there, anxiety was at a record high for me. My brain had gone into full fight or flight.

I felt almost desperate as I curled up and cried soft tears at first, then big ones. I cried until I had no more tears. I could barely move. I felt trapped in my own body. I knew my brain was in full fight/flight and I could not stop it.

Some days, I made it outside the house. Other days, fear won and I wasn't able to get out the door. Sometimes, the fear in my belly roared like a raging fire. Other days, I'd feel like I was on the verge of losing my mind. But I had an understanding of what was happening, and sufficient self-awareness to witness it happening without believing it fully. I knew I was neither the story nor the emotion, as dark as they both seemed at times. I had prepared for this. I knew what resources to use, but I had no idea it could get so intense.

At this time, PTSD felt like a life sentence. Looking at those case files for years, I had seen so many people succumb to it and never emerge on the other side of it. Yet, I couldn't shake off the feeling that maybe my body could heal. I had read incredible stories of healing. I'd met people who overcame anxiety and depression, but none had been in as deep as I had, as far as I could tell. And no one had PTSD. So doubt, bordering on despair at times, kept creeping in.

At the edge of my tolerance, wondering how it is that a body can go through so much, I retreated to the one thing that gave me hope and answers in Egypt. Prayer.

God, I am so confused and hopeless. I have seen doctors say PTSD cannot heal, but I've also seen people who supposedly couldn't heal get better. I don't know what to believe anymore. I am exhausted and almost out of hope. I can't live the rest of my life anxious like this. If a body can heal from PTSD, please show me a very clear sign. And you know I can miss signs. So, please make it so clear that even I can't miss it.

A few days later, I purchased a wellness program, and there it was. The testimony of a speaker who healed from PTSD. I couldn't believe my ears. There it was, as audible as could be, clear as the blue sky on a sunny day. PTSD can heal.

Now, I had to figure out how. Of course, I kept asking to be guided, and signs kept coming. Like breadcrumbs, I followed them right to the website of a transformational coach.

The Holism of Self-Care

Already enrolled in the program Coaching for Transformation, I was required to go through a coaching journey as a client. While browsing through the different websites, I landed on one of the faculty member's websites to find the words: "No part of us is too traumatized to heal."

Are you kidding me? A person I can speak with, and work with, knows that we can heal from trauma!

It seemed, from their methodology, that purpose exploration was a perfect path to healing. While I had found my passion in coaching, I was longing for answers to my questions: *Why am I here? And how can I contribute to the world? Why do I have to live in so many places when all I ever wanted was stability? Why does the world feel so backward to me?*

In fact, I'd been asking these questions for a while.

Back in Canada, when I was grappling with making sense of my experiences, a friend who is also a pastor said to me: "I don't know why this happened. I can't tell you why you came out of Egypt, only to fall harder than ever before. But I can tell you, I believe there is a plan for your life. It could not have been for nothing."

I wanted to believe him, but my heart had felt so broken and my faith so shaken. All I could find inside myself was doubt. And a faint hope. But the questions had kept nagging at me internally: *What if there was a purpose to it all? What if somehow this complicated, senseless journey was for something bigger? If there is a way to make sense of this, if there is a way to find the light at the end of this crazy tunnel, I want to know.*

Once again, I asked myself "If I don't do this, will I look back and regret it?" The answer was a resounding yes. And so, with doubt and deep skepticism, I embarked on the journey of exploring my purpose with my coach.

I was by no means enthusiastic, just willing to explore and hoping some answers might emerge.

> DISEMPOWERING BELIEF #6
> Self-care is selfish.

The culture of striving would have us work tirelessly. The goal is always to do more, produce more, and consume more. Our bodies are perceived as tools that are hired to deliver results paid for by employers. In this paradigm, the more we are able to work, the more we are able to deliver and, therefore, the more value we have. On the flip side, once our ability to deliver diminishes, so does our perceived value. And so we persist at jobs we don't enjoy, working in unsatisfying, difficult circumstances or even toxic environments, all because we believe that is a means to financial survival and potentially to success. In doing so, we experience stress and anxiety at astonishing levels.

According to an Everest College survey of over 1,000 individuals, 83% of US workers suffer from work-related stress. Taken to the extreme, work-related stress causes 120,000 deaths and results in $190 billion in healthcare costs yearly.[30] And it doesn't stop there—work stress affects

The Holism of Self-Care

all aspects of a person's life, hurting their job performance, disturbing their sleep, and impacting their relationships.[31]

As we saw in Chapter 2, the state of our physical bodies and health is directly related to our emotional states. Stress affects our emotions in a multitude of ways, including irritability, anxiety, mood swings, compulsive behavior, and depression.[32] To resolve this stress, we are often prescribed medication and advised to care for our bodies through exercise. Though these solutions may diminish the symptoms of stress, they do not resolve the underlying cause of the stress—an unbalanced life and unresolved emotional baggage.

Our culture encourages us to move physically and numb emotionally. In fact, most cultures discourage self-care practices due to the perception that requiring self-care is for those who are weak, sensitive, or ill. This perception naturally engages the cycle of shame and, too often, self-blame and self-sabotage. Now in addition to being physically weaker, we have invited our inner critic to the party and compounded the problem with societal shaming, giving us the perfect recipe for a downward spiral into physical and mental illness, isolation, and hopelessness.

The stagnation of unspoken and unprocessed emotion becomes psychosomatic and turns into illness over prolonged periods of time. Dr. David Servan-Shreiber writes about this extensively. His evidence-based conclusion is that while western medicine has advanced healing for infectious diseases and acute conditions, it lacks the holistic methodologies required to heal chronic diseases.[33] To compound the issue, patient care has become transactional and diagnostic in nature, rather than care based. Instead of being seen holistically, patients are seen as a combination of body parts. Dr. Brian Goldman, an Emergency Room Physician at Mount Sinai Hospital in Toronto, extensively discusses the necessity of bringing empathy into healthcare and the patient-doctor relationship through his book, *The Power of Kindness: Why Empathy is Essential in Our Everyday Lives*.[34] Until empathy and holistic care become embedded in our health care systems, we have to find the resources that can support us and build self-compassion for our healing journeys.

Breaking The Cycle

Like all other areas of our lives, our health is an area where we need to step into self-responsibility. After years of suffering from anxiety and post traumatic stress disorder, one of the most empowering moments in my journey was the day I decided to become the primary caretaker to my health and see my doctors as well-informed advisors rather than authorities with all the answers. I also made a shift to a therapist with a holistic approach.

For me, this shift happened after extensive reading on trauma-related research, the mind-body connection, and the trial of many medical and holistic modalities.

The Holism of Self-Care

Physical Self-Care

Below are some very simple facts about your biology that might allow you to see your body's functioning in a new light:

- The fight or flight stress response triggers what is called the sympathetic nervous system. This is when your body mobilizes to run from danger. Your digestive system shuts down, your heart rate increases, and your adrenal glands release adrenaline. You begin to crave sugar, coffee, smoking, and alcohol. When the stress becomes chronic, your body loses its ability to come back to a balanced state, the cravings continue, and you become more prone to headaches, intestinal problems, difficulty recovering even from exercise, memory loss, difficulty in focusing, vulnerable immune systems, and illnesses such as heart disease, anxiety, and depression.

- The activation of the parasympathetic nervous system is what allows your body to get back to a state of balance. Chronic stress causes cortisol levels to rise in your bloodstream and the body has difficulty going back to the parasympathetic nervous system function, resulting in weight gain or loss, suppressed immune systems, and digestive problems like ulcers, colitis, or irritable bowel syndrome.

- Your gut and brain are connected. Healing your gut allows your body to produce happiness hormones and healthy neurotransmitters.[35]

- When treated with appropriate care and given the resources to restore balance, your body has the ability to repair the damage it suffers from extreme stress. With recent discoveries around neuroplasticity, even the brain has been shown to be able to develop new neural pathways and heal.

The self-care required to reinstate balance in the body is at the physical, mental, emotional, and spiritual levels. I have found therapy and modern medicine to be highly effective in the acute stages of suffering with anxiety, post traumatic stress disorder, and chronic pain. Medication was also very helpful when the stress was more than my body could handle.

However, once the conditions stabilized, I reached a plateau where progress became very slow.

Perhaps the most distressing experience though was the hopeless picture painted by medicine. It seemed medication throughout my lifetime was the only available option at this stage. I had worked with disability files for a few years, and through reading hundreds of files of people with debilitating chronic illnesses, I was aware of the ramifications, and the slippery slope of increasing my medication and relying on it as the only route of treatment. In fact, I found it very strange that it was called a course of treatment given it did not truly offer a cure. It was the reason I sought alternative forms of treatment.

I recall my first appointment with a naturopath, Dr. Marie Matheson, N.D. It was with much skepticism I walked into her office, but I was at my wit's end from the lack of answers. I had been suffering from chronic pain and anxiety for years, along with the unpleasant and inexplicable symptom of pain in my lower back. It usually started in the late afternoon when my lower back would feel extremely cold. I had spoken to my doctor about it more than once, who had explained it happens to some people but wasn't indicative of anything medically speaking.

During that first appointment with Dr. Matheson, I shared my concerns with her, especially the lower back pain. Instead of suggesting it was insignificant or psychosomatic, she said that it meant my adrenal glands were drained and needed replenishing. I was stunned and very happy to hear it could be changed. After taking an herbal remedy for a couple of months, the pain subsided. To this day, Dr. Matheson remains an important resource and healer. Her practice continues to expand and the results her patients experience could be called miracles by less knowledgeable audiences.[36]

In my case, as with many friends and colleagues who had been diagnosed with depression, anxiety, or similar disorders, I resolved my symptoms outside of the primary medical explanation (or lack thereof) and with the support of doctors who were either supportive or open to me being an active part of my recovery.

Emotional Self-Care

On the emotional self-care front, once we open up to our emotions and learn to recognize our needs, we must ensure that we recognize and honor our boundaries. Beyond physical rest, emotional self-care can mean stepping away from relationships that are toxic and trigger a sense of disempowerment and pain. With time and sufficient introspection, we build healthier relationships. However, during the process, there comes a time when being focused on ourselves allows us the much-needed clarity and space for recovery before we learn to choose mutually beneficial and empowering relationships. This is not selfish. It is being responsible for our well-being and having a compassionate and heart-centered attitude towards ourselves. In turn, we will have more empathy and compassion for others, which is one of the most important skills needed to change the state of our lives and the planet.

Empathy and understanding of self are requisite to understanding others in light of the complex and interconnected world in which we live.[37] Resolving conflict and preventing misunderstanding requires us to acknowledge, respect, and understand each other's cultures, communication styles, and beliefs. Through empathy, we can avoid misinterpreting others' behaviors and bridge differences in order to find common ground and shared solutions. When empathy for others is examined in light of addiction, we find that connection and understanding are important in preventing addiction as well.[38]

Spiritual Self-Care

When working privately with clients, I am privileged to support them in making sense of their spiritual beliefs. As with any part of the coaching exploration, my role is to support them in finding their own answers. A sense of confusion, conflicts between religions, and unanswered questions lingering below the surface seem to cause many of us anguish, disorientation, and senselessness.

The Holism of Self-Care

We witness how religion, which was supposed to give us pathways to our best selves, can become a weapon of mass hatred. We see traditional explanations unable to withstand logic or out of harmony with experience. In addition to not providing some answers, religion has been used to abuse. The sense of loss we feel from this disjointed experience is profound. How do we make sense of it? How does one find clarity, consistency, stability for self, and unity with others beyond the divides created in the name of religion?

Like all other elements of our experience, there are no predefined answers. The answers lie with us. More than any other realm, our spiritual connection should come from within. This does not imply a rejection of religion. However, religion might limit the experience of connection with something larger than ourselves. Spiritual self-care is not about disconnecting from religion, nor it is about denying our discomfort and confusion. It is about bringing harmony to our beliefs, thoughts, feelings, and experience. It is about reaching spiritual maturity.

We are collectively moving from the intellectualization of religion to an experience of feeling and knowing we are connected to something bigger than ourselves. This journey requires the shedding of many layers and beliefs. It can feel very raw and vulnerable, but the alternative is staying in discomfort and confusion. Each journey is unique, and there are many paths to alignment with the essence of our connection. One general guideline I find helpful to follow is to live our process with curiosity, be honest with ourselves, and be open to hearing different perspectives, without allowing anyone to dictate or influence our process in a way we do not invite or welcome.

To cultivate this connection to something larger than yourself, you need to rely on your inner guidance—your intuition. There are many ways to connect deeper with your intuition. Unlike common misconceptions, intuition can be honed as a skill. Once you dedicate time and effort to deepening your intuition, it becomes a simple, predictable, and repeatable process. With time and practice, you learn to interpret it more accurately. In all my work with clients, connecting them with their intuition is an integral part of the coaching process because it emerges so naturally in the conversation. The more we quiet our minds and strengthen our inner witness, the more we can intuit information. The journey to living in alignment with our purpose, though mostly seen as a spiritual one, becomes more grounded and accelerates once we learn to receive our intuition. This is also how we move from left-brain functioning to whole-brain approach, relying on the intelligence of both the left and right brain to enhance the quality of our life.

While for some this process is a spiritual exploration, it is becoming increasingly grounded in science. There exist neuroscience-based methodologies to connect with intuition, whether for purposes of business growth, leadership, or inner peace. Neuroanatomist and scientist Dr. Jill Taylor describes the importance of right-brain functioning in her inspiring TED Talk, and her book, *My Stroke of Insight*. Dr. Taylor had a stroke where she lost her left-brain function and lived to recount the experience and share her insights with the world.[39]

Perhaps the best way to share the importance of intuition is to share the results of a client with whom we undertook a year-long journey of finding her purpose and bringing it to life. Today, she is a successful international coach:

"This one-year journey let me have a clearer, purer, stronger sense of who I am and what my life purpose is, which in the end has let me attract more opportunities to connect with people deeply both professionally and personally. The biggest transformation was that I do not have any fear about my work or life because now I know my purpose so well that I can select my work wisely and balance my life well."

> **PRINCIPLE #6**
> Health is best served by a holistic and preventative approach to the physical, mental, emotional, and spiritual aspects of ourselves.

Practice: Adopting a Holistic and Preventative Approach

Your well-being comes from taking a holistic approach to your life. It requires you to tend to your physical, emotional, energetic, and spiritual energy.

Some self-care practices you can incorporate into your life are:

Physical: Practice regular stretching to release tension and exercise to stay fit. Make sure you exercise in ways that you enjoy. Exercising as a chore is not sustainable, so in building the habit of exercise, make sure you like the form of exercise you use and that it fits well into the flow of your day and life.

Massages, reflexology, shiatsu, and similar forms of body treatments can be very helpful ways of releasing tension and taking care of your body.

Emotional: Meditation, naming emotions, recognizing your needs, self-awareness practices, and assertiveness are all important forms of emotional self-care. Contemplative practices, therapy, and coaching are very supportive forms of deepening self-awareness, recognizing your disempowering patterns, and creating important shifts in your life.

Energetic and Spiritual: Prayer, journaling, intuition, spiritual practices, studies, and rituals can be healing experiences that provide strength and insight. All practices impact our energetic body, yet there are specific modalities that can support energetic healing.

When you add a strong practice of self-care to your life, you live by principles of wellness and prevention, rather than illness and recovery. You become more open and available to your dreams, and less vulnerable to giving in to your fears, and inner blocks. You upgrade the quality of your internal and external life.

Well-being is the first pillar of our individual and organizational programs at Conscious Togetherness.[40]

I'd like to invite you to look at your own life and reflect on the following elements of the Life Upgrade Wheel.

The Holism of Self-Care

Life Upgrade Wheel

The Life Upgrade Wheel below is meant to guide you in assessing your current life and becoming present to the gaps between your present and your desired future.

Before filling out the wheel, create some quiet time, relax, and reflect on your life. Allow yourself to envision a future where you are happy and feeling fulfilled in all areas of your life. Do not base your answers only on today. Reflect on the last six months of your life to get a more accurate picture.

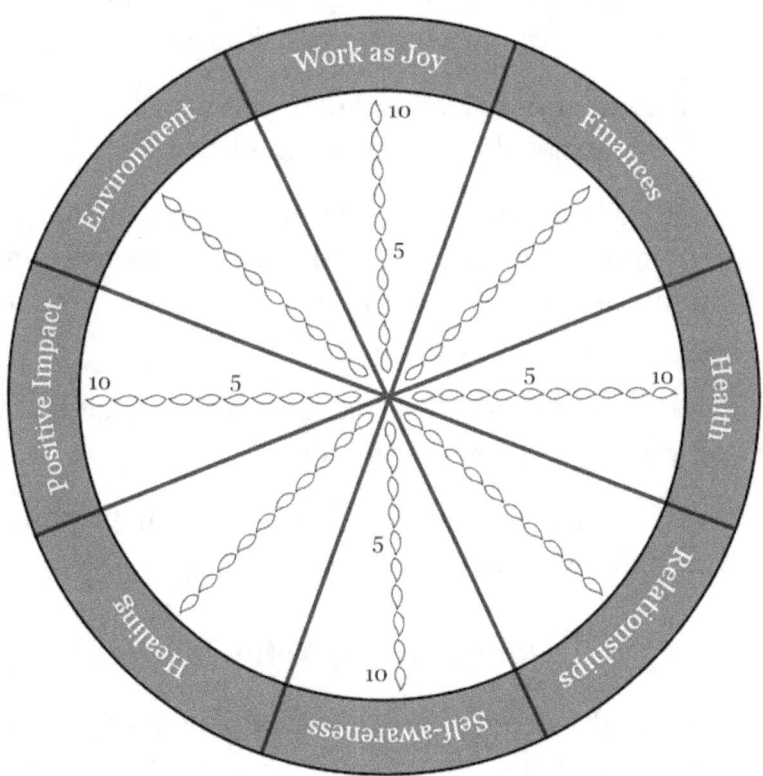

Glossary of Categories

1. **Work as Joy:** To what extent is your work an expression of your gifts, strengths, and the deliberate impact you would like to have in the world?

2. **Finances:** How would you rate your financial health, your ability to make and steward money, etc.?

3. **Health:** What is the state of your overall health—physically, emotionally, and spiritually?

4. **Relationships:** How would you rate your overall satisfaction level with the relationships in your life?

5. **Self-awareness:** How able are you to recognize your patterns of thoughts, emotions, and beliefs?

6. **Healing:** How would you rate your capacity to tune into your intuition, and heart and guide yourself through the journey of unlearning unproductive patterns and learning new productive ones?

7. **Positive Impact:** How much positive impact do you feel you have in your current life?

8. **Environment:** How would you rate your happiness with your environment?

Complete the Wheel

1. **Review the 8-wheel categories.** Think briefly about what a satisfying life would look like for you in each area. Choose a value between 1 (very dissatisfied) and 10 (fully satisfied). Use the first number that comes to mind. Do not overthink it.

2. **Draw a line that represents your satisfaction score for each area currently:** Imagine the center of the wheel is 0 and the outer edge is 10.

3. Use these questions as a guide to reflect and envision your future:
   - Which areas of your life do you need to bring balance to, and why?
   - Where do you have ease, and where it is difficult for you to create the change you desire?
   - In each of these areas, where would you like to be in 6 months, 1 year, or even 3 years?
   - What immediate actions can you commit to?

The Journey of A Healing Spirit

Am I crazy to believe there could be a purpose to life? If there is, why do so many people seem perfectly happy with not knowing it? I am so weird. What if this is all just a lie? Well, I don't have to believe any of it. I can explore it and decide for myself. It's not like the coach is asking me to believe anything. All he does is guide a process, ask questions, and share perspectives.

But I had been manipulated in the name of religion in my marriage. I had been told that I would be damned forever for saying no to my husband. For saying that I did not want to live in a marriage where I was expected to be a doormat, violated, and under constant physical, emotional, and spiritual assault. But this time, I was going to keep a sense of agency over this experience.

If I am asked to believe anything, I will stop, I promised myself. *I am willing to be open to possibilities but not having to believe anything without having my own experience validate it for me.*

One of the core principles of our coaching program was to hold people as whole. Heat rushed through me when I heard them say it.

How could they tell me I am whole when here I am unable to get through the day without feeling broken? There cannot be a way of making sense of the human experience, of the chaos of life, of illness, of injustices. If there were, why don't we all already know about it? We couldn't possibly be whole. What rubbish were they talking about? I wanted answers. Oddly enough, the very possibility of answers made me angry. I wanted to fight it. I wanted to fight and be right.

My mentor's response was very provocative: "We are all whole while simultaneously moving to a fuller experience of wholeness."

Was that supposed to be an answer?

"Stay with it," he said, answering my silent questions.

After years of exploration, I finally got it. The potential for us to live our wholeness is there. However, it can be a complicated journey to get from a sickness to wholeness.

Over the next five years, I would work with all sorts of holistic and medical modalities to get my body to heal from PTSD. I no longer require medication for anxiety or chronic pain. While some mild episodes emerge infrequently, I've learned to remain functional through them, and use them as

The Holism of Self-Care

a gateway for much deeper healing. And I've really learned that our bodies, even when sick, are a source of infinite wisdom—if only we would learn to listen to them.

Discernment, supportive medical advice, and a holistic approach are absolutely essential. I learned to see medical professionals, coaches, holistic practitioners, and energy healers as a team I create around me. Each gives me a piece of the puzzle, and I have to discern which tool, which modality, and which practitioner is the best resource for a situation.

"Our ability to reach unity in diversity will be the beauty and test of our civilization."
~Mahatma Gandhi~

CHAPTER 7

The Inevitability of Interdependence

Sitting at my desk, lost in thoughts after a call with a peer, I felt split and confused.

I recognize that I have been a victim of systemic oppression, having lost the career I dreamt of since I was a child. My life was flipped upside-down twice because of my Muslim identity in Canada, and the compounded trauma felt like it shattered my soul.

I closed my eyes and leaned my head back, hoping that shutting out my environment would help me find some internal clarity.

Despite having gone through these experiences, I cannot shake the feeling that if we approach equity and belonging work from a polarizing lens, we will be further perpetuating conflict and separation. We run the risk of repeating history rather than taking this opportunity to rise above our past and create more unity. Is there something I am missing in this conversation? What is below this confusion? I asked myself.

Opening my eyes again, I stared out the window, almost bewildered and overwhelmed by the sense of confusion and the intense feeling that I should look deeper—the nibbling sense that I couldn't just let this go. I wouldn't be able to focus on anything else.

"Rggh," I mumbled out loud in frustration.

I wish I could have more predictability in my schedule—maybe schedule when something like this drops into my emotional bin. As the thought passed through, I laughed at myself. I knew that the way to move forward was to be still and make the time to tend to the emotional disconnect, but my cultural conditioning was trying to talk me out of it. *Unconscious capitalism is alive and well in me still—the wanting to constantly "perform" so insidious that it would keep me from the only thing that will bring me peace.* So, I surrendered once more, and let go of my schedule. *It's going to be that type of day, it seems. Productivity will have to come from rest and reflection.*

Over the next few days and months, as I grappled to make sense of my experiences, noticed and released the conditioned responses that kept me confused, and deepened my learnings about systemic oppression and its impact, clarity began to emerge.

I cannot come to this conversation with a polarized approach because my life experience across cultures offers me a critical and nuanced understanding of the equity conversation.

There were many experiences in which I have received support and kindness from white people, and even systems here in Canada, while having experienced oppression and exclusion by my own family members; hence, my culture of origin.

The Inevitability of Interdependence

What part of this is internalized racism? What might be saviourism versus authentic connection and togetherness? What of my opinions is wisdom stemming from having done my healing work? I know the journey does not really end. We may be peeling back the layers of these dynamics beyond my lifetime, yet I have to acknowledge the work I have done. I have been a part of these explorations long before they suddenly came to the mainstream consciousness. I have been through the stages of grief a few times and reclaimed much of my cultural gifts from my relationship with Morocco and Canada. And while there is more work to be done, and more layers to peel, here is what I know to be true: True belonging, like power, comes from within. Waiting for others to include me perpetuates me giving them power over me. Our dynamics are universal. Their trauma is deeply embedded in our bodies, minds, and souls, not only for those on the receiving end of oppression but also for those living with the legacy of being from an oppressor group. Though at individual levels we are all impacted, some groups are significantly more impacted than others. We can be allies in shedding the oppressive impact of the systems of colonization, patriarchy, and unconscious capitalism and reclaim our individual and collective wholeness; or we can externalize the emotional and psycho-somatic impact as blame, shame, denial, and minimization. No matter which way we choose collectively, we are in this together. There is no other way.

[The previous paragraph is not an invalidation of anyone's experience or the emotional impact of their experiences. I acknowledge systemic oppression, and I caution against staying stuck in an identity of victim or persecutor.]

As these thoughts and scribblings emerged, a memory surfaced.

"Stop interrupting Kawtar. She makes some very good points." A few years ago, while on the board of a not-for-profit organization, I was the only woman of colour in the room. It was around the time I had begun reshaping my career, and I was still riddled with self-doubt about my competence, recovering from the self-depreciation I had internalized from an environment that failed to recognize the barriers I had been up against—much less, see my resourcefulness, and the opportunities I could see being someone who has lived outside the system. My voice was cracking every time I spoke; I was so busy with self-doubt and criticism that I did not even realize that every time I tried to speak, I was being interrupted. I thought I wasn't being articulate enough and blamed it on my shaky voice.

Though I had no awareness or vocabulary for what was happening in that moment, that woman naming what she witnessed and interrupting the dynamic in the room opened the door for me to find my voice. It became easier for me to speak when I was being heard. This simple observation changed everything for me. Before long, I had a total sense of belonging in the room, was contributing meaningfully, and feeling my sense of self-confidence increasing significantly. My friendships within the group deepened.

At the time, we had no language for what happened at that moment. Today, I recognize a white woman used her privileged position to interrupt a dynamic entrenched in an unconscious racist pattern. Clearly, all that was needed here was to bring the dynamic to our conscious awareness, and it stopped. Often, there is more work needed; but it wasn't so in this case.

In today's world, we have language and understanding of what happened. We can interrupt old dynamics by design. And we can do it seamlessly. Of course, given the social context, we need to build trust and learn to nuance our experiences and the stories we carry about them and our resulting interventions. And if we approach this work from our hearts, we will continually raise the bar for what it means to be human... together... instead of creating further division.

Individual and Collective Empowerment

Most people have a strong need for harmony, freedom, and self-determination. Meeting these needs allows us to embody the wholeness that we long for in our lives. While we are beginning to awaken to the personal sense of empowerment, we can create for ourselves, we can still be blind to how our dysfunctional and disempowering patterns of behaviour have been shaped by collective, inherited beliefs and patterns, and simultaneously contribute to recreating them.

The result is that we end up internalising messages about ourselves and each other that perpetuate the cycles of pain, disempowerment, dysfunction, and conflict we live in. If we are serious about creating a better life for ourselves and future generations, any examination of ourselves and our patterns without the context within which they exist remains incomplete. It keeps much of our collective ability to thrive locked away in our subconscious minds and the inherited intergenerational traumas ravaging our bodies and spirits. It wasn't enough for me to look at the beliefs that were created by the dynamics in my home; I needed to widen the scope. First, to the cultures that shaped me, to recognize how cultural beliefs played a part in my father's beliefs and behaviors, and his parents', and so on. I also had to examine the beliefs I had internalized about myself from my early years in Canada. In the same way that I found a sense of empowerment and belonging in confronting the disempowering cultural narratives that shaped my life, I found that we all have much to unlearn and shed from the disconnect between our cultural narratives, and our individual selves.

Just as we are finding our way back to our authentic and empowered selves, we are simultaneously living the same journey at a collective level. However, we have less awareness of this journey. Only in recent years is it becoming visible in our social body, and the Covid-19 era has amplified much of it for us to see. We have felt more divided and separate, and the fractures in our social fabrics have become more visible than any time before. The internal fragmentation we feel is mirrored more than ever at the social level, despite our best efforts to create a culture where everyone belongs.

How did this happen? How have we become divided in our social fabric?

As children, we learn behaviours that are deemed acceptable or unacceptable from our parents, caregivers, and teachers. Their instructions form the set of beliefs we use to navigate life until we begin to investigate the sources of our behaviour with practices like therapy, healing modalities, and other growth-oriented disciplines.

The behaviours we learn to recognize as acceptable or not (and sometimes rebel against) are not random ones; they come from generally acceptable behaviours in our culture. And while we have some awareness of our cultural values, we have little awareness of how they shape our sense of self-worth, how they contribute to our experience of empowerment or disempowerment, and how they form the collective patterns of our societies.

In other words, our beliefs about ourselves and each other are shaped by our culture. Culture is like the invisible water we swim in. It determines behaviours that are considered good and those that are considered bad, and thereby the people who we perceive as good and people we perceive as bad. We then project that onto groups because our brain likes to categorize things to help us navigate the physical world and find our "place" in it. Just as we hold disempowering stories as individuals, we hold disempowering stories as groups of people. To the extent that we hold these stories to be true, they dictate who we should like, who we should trust, who we see as good, who we see as bad, and how we should treat each of these people. These stories are imprinted in our subconscious minds by our cultures. They impact not only how we see others, but also how we see ourselves. They impact our connection to our inner power and our chances of experiencing success in life. These are our cultural values and norms that we then begin to project on each other, creating separation and division. While culture's goal is to organize our lives, it inevitably creates polarization.

Cultural conditioning amplifies and accelerates our natural human tendency to fear the unfamiliar and different. It goes back to that outdated internal programming designed to keep us safe, and which triggers the fight, flight, and freeze response. For most of us, others are still unknown, and the unknown is deemed a threat until proven otherwise. We are naturally wired to be biased against those we perceive as others. Yet, when our perception remains unchecked, we create an "us" versus "them" dynamic, where we are right and they are wrong; then we justify holding them apart, attacking them, hurting them, terrorizing them, or killing them. We fail to recognize and own about ourselves that, too often, what we are fighting is the fear of the unknown and the perception of the other, rather than their reality.

Just like we carry our personal stories, we carry collective stories. Many of these narratives are below the surface of our conscious mind and hold the limits of what we believe to be possible as a collective, our beliefs about what we can or cannot do, reminders of our inherited alliances and enemies, and tales of those who are "good" and those who are "bad"— which identities have access to resources and which ones do not, and who is considered inherently worthy and less worthy of having. As long as these stories remain unspoken and unexamined, they remain in our collective unconscious and colour our interactions with the world.

The Inevitability of Interdependence

The Culture Iceberg

Perceived by the five senses

Easy to see, hear, touch, taste, and smell

Art

Places of Worship

Food

Dance Architecture

National and Regional Clothing

Deep-rooted beliefs about

Boundaries Age Hierarchy

Faith/Religion Time Friendship

Justice Communication Conflict

Leadership Status Destiny

Gender Roles Tradition

Money

Deeper layers of beliefs and values dictating behaviors

Require awareness of self and environment

An Example: The Gender Polarity

Although the beliefs that we use to justify separation and polarization have now been proven incorrect, our subconscious belief in separation, along with our unexamined fears, traumas, biases, and narratives perpetuate the "othering" we inflict on each other.

Let us examine the traditional men vs. women polarity that has plagued our societies for centuries, and still does in many cultures today, not as a way to justify blaming and shaming but to illustrate and awaken to the speed at which we have moved (or failed to move) in the past from unconscious bias, to aligned, conscious action.

For many centuries, gender roles between men and women were rather rigid. Men were taught to be strong and play the role of providers while women were taught to be caregivers and homemakers. Women were neither encouraged nor supported to play an active part in society beyond the household or caring professions. They have been taught to be followers rather than leaders, implementers rather than thinkers.

Men have been the center of economic and political power in this model. And while they have benefited from this privilege, the reality is that it has been toxic and highly destructive for men, and all of society, to be boxed into a role that requires them to shut out the emotional and creative parts of themselves. As a result, male leaders are largely disconnected from the people they are leading. It should be no surprise that men are in a crisis of isolation and loneliness, resulting in the highest rates of male suicide in many countries like the USA, UK, Japan, and many more.[41] The ever-increasing pressure

The Inevitability of Interdependence

to perform without an acknowledgment of the humanity of each individual, and without tools for well-being, is a recipe for disaster.

While a rigid division of roles might have made sense in previous centuries for our species to survive, in our current times, it has become a hindrance to us reaching a higher ground; it has, in fact, become a powerful tool of divide and suffering.

The reality is that investment in women and gender parity improves the health, education, and economic conditions of entire communities. Relative to men, women devote a greater proportion of their earnings to investing in family, resulting in better health outcomes for both themselves and their children.[42] Communities in which girls and women achieve higher levels of education have better labor force participation and smaller families, allowing them to save and invest more. Families are then able to be self-sufficient, and communities and governments are able to spend on improving infrastructure and projects that promote further economic growth.[43]

In business, women are consistently perceived to be better at soft leadership skills than men—they treat their teams more equitably, demonstrate greater adaptability, manage conflict better, mentor and coach their teams, value diversity, and consider social impact.[44,45] Studies have shown that the greater the number of women in senior executive levels, the more profitable the firm.[46] Despite this, skills and traits where women have the greatest advantage over men are perceived as less important in public surveys, even though empathy is the most critical soft skill for effective leadership, allowing leaders to build relationships, enhance creativity, and improve employee engagement.[47]

Even in peacebuilding, research shows that peace agreements are 35% more likely to last when women are an integral part of the negotiation process.[48] This is because, in politics, women demonstrate greater compassion and empathy resulting in better compromises. Improved gender parity means political stability and reduces the likelihood of violent conflict. Empathy is not exclusive to women, however. It is a part of the right brain skills, yet women have more access to it, likely because they are socialized to be empathetic and caring. It is imperative that in using the gender example, we do not become entrenched in seeing it as men versus women. In fact, many women with a high need for power perpetuate toxicity.

In a recent research study, Birsu Karaarslan, a student at the Graduate Institute Geneva examined the role of women in rebuilding Rwanda after the genocide.[49] The post-genocide Rwanda was an arid land with its people left deeply traumatized. Men were the majority of the victims who died, leaving the society 70% female after the genocide. Women then found themselves having to rebuild their communities in the aftermath. Having relied predominantly on an agricultural economy, women had to feed their communities, sell food, and care for their orphans, all while carrying the deeply traumatic burden and memory of the genocide. With a population of 70%, women became the center of the economy and society. They organized to end the war and achieve peace while promoting reconciliation, reconstruction, and forgiveness. In 2001, the government introduced the 3-ballot method, ensuring 30% of the parliamentary seats were devoted to women while making sure that youth were also represented. By 2008, 56% of parliamentary seats were women and by 2012, women were running 43% of the businesses in the country. Hence, Rwanda became the first African country to be closer to achieving the Millennium Development Goals. It was also ranked 5th in the global gender equality index in 2016, which was a significant shift from the situation before the genocide.

Despite ample evidence that reverses our bias against women in leadership roles at all levels cognitively, deeper mindset and policy shifts lag behind.

> *DISEMPOWERING BELIEF #7*
> *We are separate from others.*

American educator Jane Elliott, in her experiment "Blue eyes, Brown eyes" shows how we learn to be divided and treat each other with prejudice.[50] She does so by giving her students a belief that they are better because of the colour of their eyes. As we watch the experiment, we can see the impact of a belief on actions. We are collectively carrying centuries of such beliefs, hidden deep in our psyche and its trauma held in our cellular memory.

I began to recognize that much of my conditioned behaviour as a young professional came from my conditioning as an Arab woman and the role of the good girl. As I had been taught, my role was to keep the peace by staying quiet about the dysfunctional and abusive patterns I was dealing with. However, while the same identity of being a woman allowed me to access some sense of personal power in Canada as my healing journey continued, the identities of being Arab and Muslim were ones that justified my oppression and exclusion. Systemically, one identity was acknowledged as marginalized and was supported; but the others were seen as a threat, and the bias towards my competence, my abilities, and justified treating me as less than other Canadians.

This is how our cultural values and social systems become embedded with the beliefs that dictate our individual and structural behaviours and policies. Once again this is nuanced as within a country, we find several sub-cultures and groups of people. And a simple analysis of our context is not sufficient to bring us out of the paradigms of separation. We have to recognize that none of us are a group. We carry some characteristics of the groups we belong to and combine that with our own individual make-up. This is why two people with the same general characteristics from the same culture will go through the same experience and yet emerge with two different subjective realities of the impact of the experience.

> *At the core of the fragmented approaches we use to recreate the dynamics of oppression is a belief that we are independent of each other. We seem to have suffered a collective amnesia about our interdependence.*

The Inevitability of Interdependence

When we are functioning from the paradigm of independence, we are acting from deep-seated beliefs that we have to compete for resources and safety, therefore justifying to ourselves our impulses to control, extract, compete and exploit each other.

The real disconnect created by the belief that we are independent of each other is that it allows us to move through our lives caring only about pieces instead of the whole. We fail to recognize that in believing we are separate, we perpetuate violence, believing it will not affect us or those we care about. But if we realize that this fragmented worldview is an illusion that hurts us both internally, and externally, we might begin to recognize that there is no "other," and therefore that *we are all responsible for the whole.*

This thought can be daunting at first, and because of that, we try to reject it, especially for those of us raised in individualistic cultures. If you are a reader from an individualistic culture, more than any other chapter, this chapter is likely to be the one you find challenging your worldview. Because it challenges a basic assumption on which individualism thrives, and hence is deeply embedded into your psyche. Wherever you are from, however, you will read this chapter through your lenses, your cultural conditioning, and lived experiences–just as I write it through mine. There is a powerful opportunity as you read to notice your conditioning. If you find resistance or strong emotions happening within you as you read, I invite you to pause and acknowledge how you feel. And to remember that I do not ask you to believe anything in this book. Rather, I offer you perspectives that you are at choice to engage with from curiosity, or reject; and both are okay. I want to remind you here that I offer my perspective and lens, informed by my life experiences, not an absolute truth, but rather my truth. Instead of looking to agree or disagree with this content, the best way you can have it serve your journey is to mindfully engage in the reading and exploration, as a commitment to your own growth; and explore the questions at the end with curiosity, and ideally with people from different backgrounds.

I believe humanity longs for coherence, for an experience of harmony, an experience of connection across our differences. And I believe this to be simultaneously the noblest and self-serving endeavour we undertake for our survival as a species. I also believe we are in an evolutionary process that is calling us, through our current challenges, to move from survival to thriving. So, in my eyes, we are living at a pivotal time in history where we are facing our biggest opportunity to leap and offered our darkest challenges as a doorway. In the same way our individual growth reaches pivotal phases, so does our collective growth. And this is how we find ourselves in this collective dark night of the soul.

If we want to create a brighter future for all, a society where everyone can thrive, it is time to revisit the unexamined assumptions we hold about other identities, acknowledge them, and broaden our examination to all the sources of divides within our societies. We will need to make a conscious and brave effort to move from thinking from *separation* and step into thinking from *wholeness*. One of the most powerful shifts we can make is to recognize that in separation thinking, we in fact all lose; and when we act holistically, we reduce suffering for everyone and the strain on our planet. We step into coherence.

The Inevitability of Interdependence

Breaking The Cycle

What is coherence?

Coherence is the idea that the universe is composed of interconnected and dynamic networks of biological structures and processes and has been one of the great scientific findings of the 20th century.[51] People are not independent of each other. In a coherent system, the parts are related to the whole, which is a part of a greater whole, which is again a part of something greater. We, our emotions, and our actions not only impact those we interact with, but also our families, our communities, society, and the world. Coherence reinforces an individual's ability to have outsized influence on a broader level. As people learn to self-regulate and achieve individual coherence, their enhanced intuition, positive energy, and newfound balance will have a beneficial impact on the interconnected whole. This effect will extend into social and eventually global coherence, where the entire system is in a state of balance.

Interestingly, brain studies show that traditionally masculine traits of competition, linearity, and boldness are associated with the function of the left brain; and, traditionally, feminine traits such as empathy, collaboration, and recognition of interconnectedness are associated with the functions of the right brain. Working with only one severely hinders your ability to live wholeheartedly, create well-being in your life, achieve win-win outcomes, and connect with creative solutions to complex issues. Research shows the future of leadership to be one of whole-brain leadership.[52] Yet, only 8% of today's leaders use whole-brain leadership in their companies. That means up to 92% of decision-making in our world is happening from a limited line of thinking, one that often does not take into account the needs of communities and whole systems. Is it any wonder our world is in a dire state of separation, and we are collectively experiencing anguish and imbalance?

I spent many years learning from Eastern wisdom and combining it with Western methodologies and teachings. From temple stays where I learned from Buddhist monks in South Korea, to the wisdom of archetypes and goddesses in Hindu traditions, to Joseph Campbell's Hero's Journey, and Marian Woodman's Death Mother, I synthesized my learning to create the Conscious Togetherness Leadership Framework®. The resulting expansion allows us to deal with complex issues and make decisions for the benefit of all stakeholders.

I have found in my life and work that shifting from a fragmented life to a holistic one is considerably simpler than we might expect and can be cultivated through the set of practices suggested in this book. It is by seeing life from a higher perspective that we recognize patterns of the utmost importance. These patterns can be found in Carl Jung's archetypes, in mythology, and in elevating religious teachings from a literal sense. There are misconceptions that this journey makes us soft and unable to perform. The reality, however, is that this journey opens you up to the peaceful possibilities of life. We learn to listen to our intuition and the flow of life around us. We integrate parts of ourselves, and thus, contradictions we struggle with about the world. Through this, we discover the path of least resistance where we get more done with less effort. (In the podcast, Listening

The Inevitability of Interdependence

To Restore Peace After Disruption, Nienke van Bezooijen, Dr. Scilla Elworthy, and I share ways and practices for listening to self, others, and the world, a necessary first step to create balance.)[53]

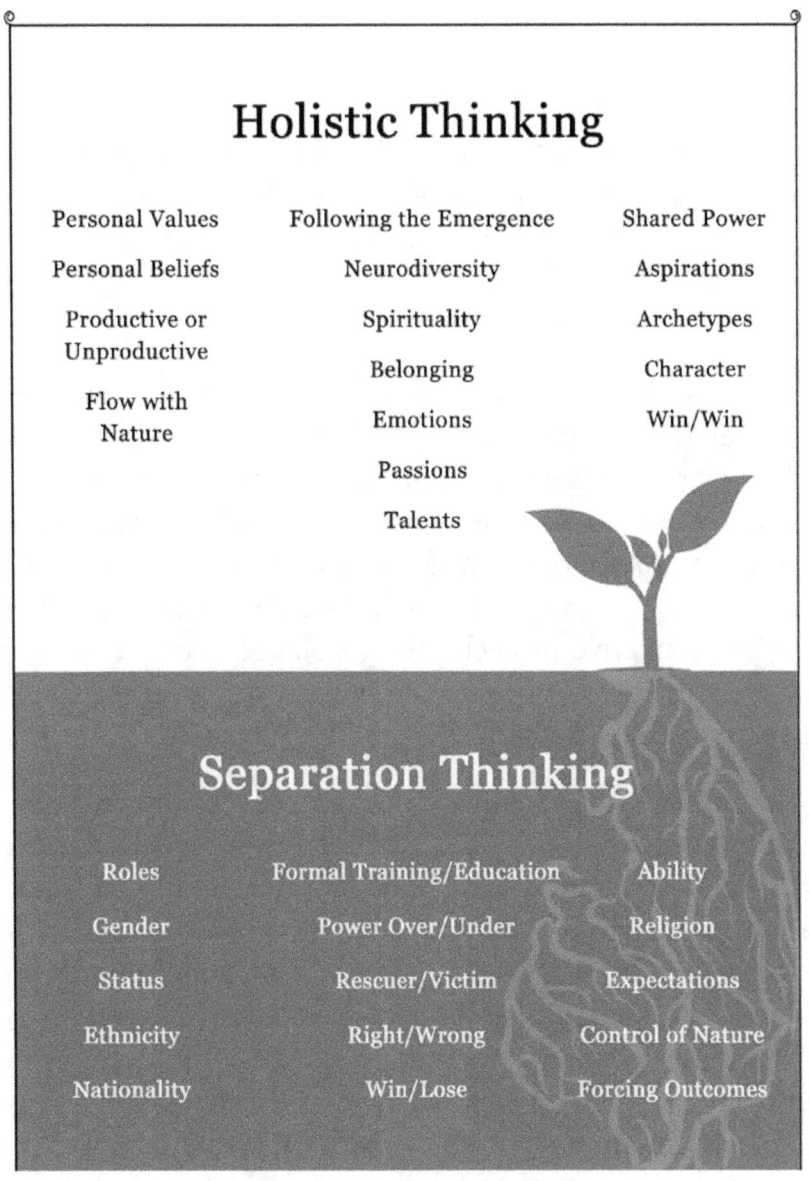

Holistic Thinking

Personal Values	Following the Emergence	Shared Power
Personal Beliefs	Neurodiversity	Aspirations
Productive or Unproductive	Spirituality	Archetypes
	Belonging	Character
Flow with Nature	Emotions	Win/Win
	Passions	
	Talents	

Separation Thinking

Roles	Formal Training/Education	Ability
Gender	Power Over/Under	Religion
Status	Rescuer/Victim	Expectations
Ethnicity	Right/Wrong	Control of Nature
Nationality	Win/Lose	Forcing Outcomes

This holistic perspective elevates our vision from seeing each other through the current lenses of separation, to making sense of the chaos and recognizing the collective's role in each person's life, as well as each person's role in the larger collective.

> *Acknowledging and creating harmony with our diversity will allow us to capitalize on our differences and create richness in our lives rather than conflict.*

If it wasn't for moral imperatives, research provides us with evidence that diversity profits the bottom line and allows for more creative solutions.[54] On the opposite end of this spectrum, we remain stuck in a singular narrative and worldview. As writer Chimamanda Ngozi Adichie shares in her TED Talk, we risk remaining stuck in a singular and limited narrative of each other.[55] She goes on to link the single narratives to power and how stories have the power to connect us or dehumanize us.

As a professional certified coach, and coach trainer, I have the privilege of unpacking issues of power, privilege, rank, culture, and identity with leaders of diverse backgrounds. From the richness of this tapestry emerges the possibility to sit together, beyond polarity, to recognize and acknowledge our shared humanity and interdependence. To process the impact of systems and cultural heritage built on exclusion and othering. It is an opportunity to heal collectively and co-create a new empowering story with each other. We work to unpack the impact of social identities, to move from power over and under to power with, and power within. From using only the left-brain skills, to balancing the left and right brain functions for whole-brain, values- and purpose-driven leadership.

The Power of Holistic Leadership

Holistic leadership is one that brings the masculine and feminine attributes of each person into balance. A more scientific view of it is whole-brain leadership. My dear friend and collaborator, Nienke van Bezooijen, connects leaders with their authentic voices to speak on world stages. She has been balancing the feminine and masculine through her work with leaders for many years. She shares with us the following case study:

Breakthrough to the Feminine

In my work as a speaker coach, it's my purpose to help people express their true voice. To balance the masculine and feminine element is an integral part of finding that voice. I remember Harry, an established male of fifty-eight, asked to give a TEDx talk. His first draft of his talk was all about his career. He just stepped back voluntarily from his position as CEO of a large international company. His motto was, 'There is a time for learning, earning, and returning." When he shared that, I felt the space to get him out of his thinking mode and make a bridge to the deeper expressed feminine. 'Til then, I only heard about his impressive career steps, the important network he had built, and his position at the social ladder he enjoyed very much.

The opening to space from thinking to the heart is often the question: "Why are you doing what you are passionate about?"

At that moment, I asked the question and he became quiet, stared a while in front of him, and then answered: "I grew up in a little village—beautiful nature near the coal mines. But we weren't allowed to play near one creek. It would kill us, my mom told me. I remember standing beside the water, so clear and precious. How could that kill us? And if I was able to do so, I declared it at that moment at the age of seven years, to stop the pollution and dedicate my life to saving the planet!"

This question I asked, getting from the head into the heart, shifted his life. In all his public speaking, he now includes the Harry of seven years old too. His "returning to the world" stage of his life got a whole new dimension, and he loves it! For me, it's the joy of seeing in my clients' eyes the spark, the clicking moment of balancing the masculine and the feminine we all have.

The Personal and The Systemic

Just as coherence has shown that we are in fact interconnected, we are at a time when we can see the interdependency we have with our systems. The decisions we make in our daily lives impact the systems that govern and rule our lives. And vice-versa.

We are awakening to the painful reality that the systems we have collectively created are in our image—highly imperfect, perpetuating separation and exclusion. While changing

The Inevitability of Interdependence

systems can seem overwhelming or intimidating, the reality is that every action from any part of a system impacts the whole. The following chapter speaks more to the power and responsibility we each hold as a member of a larger collective. My dear friend and mentor, Vikram Bhatt, is the Founder of Leadership That Works India, a global coaching organization where we teach coaching with a systemic lens.[56] In the interview with Christopher Mc Auliffe, Vikram shares how we can create new and inclusive systems through an evolutionary lens.[57] While the interview is about the coaching profession, the principles apply to all fields.

The good news is that actions, as simple as ensuring we are living from well-being, contribute meaningfully to those around us, and those far from us. What seems like a selfish act benefits the whole. This is the nature of healthy interdependency. When we take radical self-responsibility for our lives, we inevitably contribute meaningfully to the whole.

> **PRINCIPLE #7**
> *Moving from separation to wholeness is essential to create a more gentle, connected, and peaceful world.*

Practice: From Separation to Interdependence and Wholeness

1–Individual and Collective Impact

Growing up in a disconnected world means you learned to experience yourself in disconnected ways. You likely feel something is missing in your life, internally and externally. Wholeness is a journey of reorganizing the way you learned to experience the world beyond fragmentation, and therefore the foundations on which you base decisions.

This week, I invite you to reflect on where you are acting from separation thinking and where you are operating from holistic thinking, as well as the emotional impact of that thinking on yourself and others.

Impact on You

Reflect on times when you felt excluded due to separation thinking and retrace the emotional impact of the experience on you.

Where are you being excluded or marginalized due to your identities? If you have not had exposure to this work before, I suggest you begin by reflecting on how you find yourself not fitting in? What makes you different and makes you stand out? Here are some specific examples below:

Think about your social identities:

- What is your gender of birth? How do you identify with regard to gender?
- What is your nationality and ethnicity?

The Inevitability of Interdependence

- What sub-group are you from in your country or region?
- What is your age?
- Are you primarily a feeler or intuitive who finds it hard to fit in with the heavy left-brain-focal culture?
- Are you from a marginalized identity? What opportunities have been difficult or unattainable for you that others around you were able to access?
- What is your profession? Did you choose it because it makes your heart sing or for financial safety, or because it was the expectation of your parents? What beliefs did you internalize about your ability to earn from what you love?

For each of these experiences, write down how you feel and what you believed about yourself because the world mirrored it to you. You can refer to the lists of emotions in Chapter 2 to name the impact with precision.

Keep track of what you notice around your identities next week.

Impact on Others

Write a list of groups you have heard biases against in your life. In each culture, we hear negative messages about groups. It can be in your own community, or from your parent's background if you don't live where your parents grew up.

Put aside any blame and shame, and write these down. You are bringing to your awareness important messages you internalized about others. Once you write these down, answer the following questions:

- How have you treated others as a result of these beliefs?
- Are there people whose opinions you made less valuable?
- Are there people you believe are less competent because they studied in other cultures, or others that you deem more competent than you because they went to specific schools?
- Sitting in a public park, notice who you feel scared of when you see people? Is there a commonality you see? Who do you trust by default?

Bring to mind a time that you interacted with someone from separation thinking or bias and you were proven wrong.[58]

What did you learn from the experience?

What will you do differently as a result?

2–A Social Experiment

In the field of intercultural training, we learn to interact with other cultures from a set of cultural dimensions that create distinctions to give us frames of understanding each other, with curiosity rather than perpetuate value judgments of different cultures. This paradigm shift moves us from cultural superiority or inferiority to cultural humility and openness.

Expatriates often share the experience of living in a foreign environment and seeing the butterfly effect of decisions; and yet their interdependence with locals makes them

The Inevitability of Interdependence

seek connection, understanding, and friendships with the local community, as different as it may be from their own culture. Though these experiences do not generally examine the power dynamics and privilege at play, with increased awareness, I believe expatriates are a group that could be pioneering unity across divides in the world.

The example I share below is one from my experience as an expatriate. It demonstrates how our beliefs about each other either open or close our hearts to each other, therefore, creating separation and division.

The Joy of Interconnection

Staring at the package, I could not figure out whether this was salt or sugar.

Ugh, why do these little things have to be so hard? I wondered as I looked up to locate someone in the supermarket who might speak English. No luck.

For what felt like the millionth time in the last six months, I felt like a helpless child—unsure of the simplest things. Tears swelled in my eyes.

What am I doing here? What did I come here for? I knew this was going to be hard. What if I made a big mistake? Should I go back home?

I wanted to put down the package, run back to our apartment, pack my bags, and fly home. Instead, I took deep breaths, took mindful steps towards the cash register, bought the mystery package, and went home to find out it was sugar.

Gahhh! I was trying to buy salt.

Looking around at the big inviting kitchen, it all felt cold. I felt cold.

I hate being here. I wanna go home. I can't keep feeling so lost and disconnected. I cannot be here for three years like this. Something has to change. But what? How?

It was so overwhelming to start everything anew here in South Korea and help my daughter and husband to cope with their new lives, too. I did my best to make the home and the transition as comfortable as possible, but there was very little comfort in it. There was very little joy. It felt like coping was all there was.

Of course, that's not exactly true. I was living in a very different place from anything I had known. My life was a blank canvas. I had chosen to be here. And, speaking with other ex-pat parents, I knew I was not the only one. And I knew about the adjustment cycle. *I am at the most critical edge—six months. I have to turn this around. What can I do to make this easier?*

Suddenly, a lightbulb moment. *Gratitude!*

Back in Canada, while I was on sick leave, I had started a gratitude journal. *Surely, there are things I can be grateful for, even if I feel like there aren't.*

The Inevitability of Interdependence

> *While emotions are a guide, when they become a way of being, they can also become a trap.*

I knew this to be true; and practicing a simple, grounded gratitude exercise daily had helped me shift my perspective in the past. So, I started my gratitude practice again.

I began to see things I felt grateful for but was disregarding because everything felt like a fight internally. One of the things I was most grateful for was a new friendship with a Korean friend I had met, who would later become a friend, mentor, and colleague, who had allowed me to have some deep and authentic conversations about my experiences. Through her, I had found out more about South Korea, its history, its present state. And its beauty.

The words of my Korean teacher in Canada reverberated through my mind as I wrote about my friend. "They will love you because you are a lawyer and married to a diplomat. But they will not like you because you are brown and fat." I realized that belief had closed me off to the potential of the experience. I had already decided that I would not be liked and could not make local friends.

But clearly, that is not true. I wonder what else isn't true?

Through the study of non-violent communication and cultural dimensions, I had learned that we have universal needs, and I was wondering how to connect with a culture that felt so different.

Suddenly, the next lightbulb moment.

A social experiment.

I started smiling at random strangers on the subway. At first, they would often ignore me, or look surprised or annoyed. But after a few attempts, I noticed they looked back after looking away. And when they looked back, they would often smile back. And that's when it would happen—the sense of joy and connection would fill me from the heart outward.

I loved proving myself wrong. See, we are all just humans going about our lives, unsure whether to trust those who are different. Yet clearly, all it takes is a kind heart and a willingness to meet the other. This simple experiment showed me the power of letting go of my bias and opening my heart to others. And I went on to meet many wonderful, warm, and kind Korean people.

A little gratitude and a social experiment, and I was back from the precipice of disconnection and frustration. What if, sometimes, it could be that easy?

"If you think you are too small to have an impact, try sleeping with a mosquito."
~The Dalai Lama~

CHAPTER 8

The Relief of Self-Leadership

"I am actively doing my healing work. But I am tired. How long does this continue?" my friend and peer asked at the close of our coaching session.

"As long as it takes. We do not get to decide when a cycle closes, or when the healing has occurred. We just find things different. That amazing moment when we are faced with the same pattern, and we find within ourselves a different response. Without effort, without pain. Just a different response." The words flowed out of me, even though I'd never really thought about this before that moment.

"In the meantime, I want to invite you to be compassionate with yourself. You have demonstrated so much strength and that has always helped you come out the other side stronger. You are a leader, my friend. This is just the beginning"

"You're right. It's better than it's been before, and it's only getting better." She paused, letting the awareness sink in. "Thanks, Kawtar. I have to run now, but I'm going to journal about this and follow up with you tomorrow."

I spent my life interacting with the world from the victim's lens and judged myself for it for a long time. And suddenly, I am just accepting it? I am no longer ashamed of it?

In this conversation with my friend, I realized I could now own even this truth about myself.

I have found the strength to face the hardest truth about my life. And I have navigated every adversity with a commensurate dose of courage. Instead of falling into the old cycle of self-blame and self-shame, I can now start my inquiry with the question: How am I giving my power away here? I have become the leader of my life, instead of a follower, defaulting to every pattern and story that was written for me.

When we hung up, I sat in my chair, looking around my home office, staring at my beautiful vision board.

What a milestone! This is one of my proudest moments.

I could feel the liberation and leadership pulsing through my veins.

DISEMPOWERING BELIEF #8
We need others to take action for us.

We Are the Leaders We Have Been Waiting For

When you look at the world around you, who do you see as leaders? What makes you see them as such?

I grew up in a world where leadership was defined by gender and seniority. For a long time, I thought this was only the case in cultures similar to mine. It came as a shock to me when I found out that even in western countries, leadership is still

The Relief of Self-Leadership

very much position- and status-based. As I moved between Eastern and Western cultures, I found that, in practice, leadership most often refers to authority. This leadership paradigm gives responsibility and authority to a minority of people, entrusting them to create "desired" outcomes for communities while the majority follows instructions and executes.

In this model of leadership, we delegate responsibility to others to manage critical aspects of our lives: health and well-being, policies and programs, and important decisions that impact our communities. In a culture where this model is the norm, we often grow up assuming that we do not have the skills or the character to lead. We simply delegate and live with the consequences of delegating our lives. We even believe we are too small and insignificant to make an impact. We worry that if we were to make decisions, we would make mistakes, feel guilt, or get blamed. All these are disempowering beliefs that keep us from being active citizens and leaders—from using our two most powerful tools for change: our voice and choice.

This delegation has resulted in a situation where our well-being is secondary to an unjustified need for constant economic growth, our health is in the hands of companies, our water and land are increasingly toxic, and our communities are torn and polarized. The answers are always out of our reach, while we ride the merry-go-round of making enough money to care for our family's basic needs, pay down debt, afford health care, or purchase the next trendy gadget. Focused on our daily merry-go-round, we deem the bigger issues of the world, not ours to solve.

The world can be overwhelming and the issues facing our time are certainly complex. Expecting others to find solutions is both the comfortable and conditioned response. But consider this: If we all continue waiting for others to lead, where does it leave the urgent problems with which our world is grappling? Where does it leave the future of our planet and the generations inheriting the problems we created?

> *If we are not proactively shaping our lives, we are living as victims of circumstances, of others' decisions, of systems that we delegated power to, often without sufficient accountability.*

The truth is, whether we realize it or not, we are all leading. Our life is the platform of our leadership. As we move from the old paradigms and the ideas keeping us stuck, we step into Self-leadership —a way of life where we awaken to our ability to impact situations and outcomes, where our personal and collective responsibility and power are no longer separate. Not only through chance, but by design. This is the big difference between the old paradigm and the new paradigm.

Due to the interconnected nature of our world, each action we take impacts the world in some way. Each product we buy gives validation to its manufacturers, their values, and the way they treat their workforce. Each interaction we have leaves a person feeling smaller or better. This is the reason why "being" practices like meditation, introspection, self-inquiry, and shifting perspectives are important. Before making any impact through our doing, we make it through our being.

> With the interconnected nature of our world, every inner shift you experience and every action you take (or do not take) impacts the collective.

Dr. Jane Goodall sums it up in her quote: "You cannot get through a day without having an impact. What you do makes a difference, and you get to decide what kind of difference you want to make." Only right now, our impact is happening by default. Most of us are not proactively choosing it and interrupting the patterns that perpetuate it.

Beginning to see your life as your impact platform awakens you to the opportunity of impacting your family and community with intentionality. You can invest your energy toward what you truly desire and what enhances the world.

> Moving to a paradigm of Self-leadership is about consciously shifting the places where the impact you have is incongruent with the world you would like to live in, understanding that no shift is too small and no action is too little.

This is what I call leadership by influence, a powerful option for those who are not willing or do not have a desire to lead by authority. The weight of leadership roles, the decision-making required, and the fear of making mistakes or misusing one's own power can all deter the best leaders from stepping into formal leadership roles. Recognizing that each decision you make contributes to shaping the larger tapestry of life means you are responsible for your impact and aware that you are leading by influence when you are not leading by authority. Even when you are not the ultimate decision-maker, you can steer your energy towards influencing outcomes. This is particularly important and true of environments with rigid structures of power.

While we may associate formal leadership with authority, the leadership required for the 21st century is no longer limited to technical or management skills. The new paradigm in leadership is about being willing to admit what is not working, inquire with integrity, address problems from curiosity, implement changes, adjust, and improve to ensure the solutions are holistic for the communities we serve and the environmental imprint. This new paradigm of leadership requires courage, integrity, authenticity, openness, intuition, flexibility, care, and compassion for all forms of life, present and future.

I define leadership as the ability to commit to a meaningful pursuit and direct time, energy, and resources to achieving its highest outcome for everyone involved, as well as the environment. What is leadership for you?

Take a moment to reflect on your relationships, your community, and the issues that matter most to you.

What kind of impact are you currently having in each of these areas?

The Relief of Self-Leadership

What kind of impact would you like to have?

What is stopping you from getting there?

The diagram below shows the continuum of Stages of Self-leadership. Where the old leadership model was about authority and delegation, the new paradigm is about recognizing how to put our own strengths, skills, and purpose in service to a meaningful pursuit. With most of our basic needs met, meaning and purpose are becoming increasingly important in our lives. This means leadership is becoming self-driven, because it requires us to act on our internal drive, on issues that matter to us as an individual, in partnership with organizations or individuals working toward a common purpose and a shared vision. This is precisely the reason why contemplative practices and right-brain skills are more important now than ever. We are moving from living and working with an external compass and set of rules, to aligning our left-brain skills of strategy and execution in service to our inner calling and vision. This shift can be disorienting for many leaders, and there is often a phase of feeling lost and confused without a roadmap to navigate it.

Where the old model required leaders to believe they had the answers, the new one requires us to acknowledge the reality that we do not have the answers and then make peace with the fact that aligned action emerges through exploration rather than through the linear mind. In this sense, we can only make way for new solutions once we acknowledge that the current ones have been insufficient and inefficient in solving the challenges we face. Combining the power of our right brain with our left brains in this way allows us to tap into new possibilities, from a place of flow, hence least resistance.

The case studies below show the journeys of three individuals who are leading in this way and the impact they are having on their communities. While in the past, we may have looked up to leaders we saw as exceptional believing they were luckier, today we have the tools to bring out the best in each of us by design.

Stages of Self-leadership

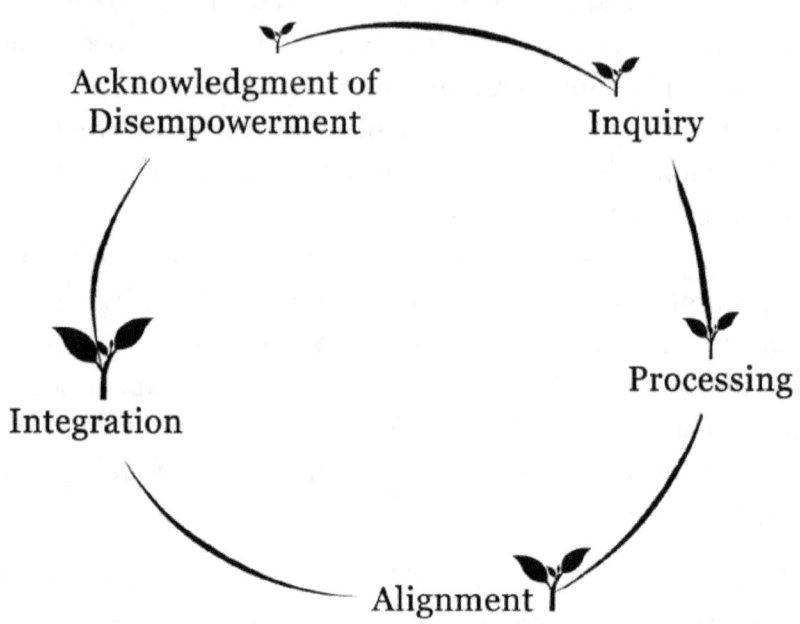

Breaking The Cycle

There are many examples in the world of ordinary people tackling large issues. These individuals inspire me deeply and show us that ordinary people can have an extraordinary impact. To me, these people live by the markers of a purposeful life, even though many of them struggle to describe how they create such an impact. They talk about following an inner nudge, a calling, but they are not able to give us a roadmap for this change. I remember this feeling of awe and simultaneous frustration when I used to read stories of inspiring figures. Only a few select people seemed to have answers, yet they remained scattered across different disciplines. Over the last few years, I have studied and experimented intensely with the practices and methodologies that empower us to align ourselves with the impact we long to create in the world. I no longer see these as random occurrences, but rather as the result of a mindset and practices that culminate in alignment with one's purpose.

Case Studies of Real-life (S)Heroes

Shero 1

Urja Shah is the President of Setco Foundation in Mumbai, India, and the CSR Director for the Setco Group of companies, India. Urja loves art and design; and from the start of her professional journey, she was motivated by making agency and self-determination accessible to India's textile artisans— the bearers of India's art and craft heritage. She aspired to not only preserve the high quality of craftsmanship amongst the textile artisans, but also to empower weavers, embroiderers, and other craftspersons financially. After graduating from Duke University and Parsons School of Design, Urja returned to Mumbai and started her own bridal design boutique. Her core values of preserving tradition, supporting those who work with her, and empowering others financially expressed themselves in the core values of her studio. She strove to ensure that her employees had access to fair compensation, training and professional development, education, and avenues for pursuing their dreams. Her passion and joy expressed themselves in co-designing with families and brides-to-be in a way that represented the bride's choice but also aligned with the values of the collective and her studio. When the business scaled, Urja felt that she had lost the real connections at the heart and purpose of her design work. As she felt disconnected from the essence of her work, her discontent grew; and she decided to take a break to re-align. From a purpose lens, this was Urja's first cycle of purpose coming to an end. It was a difficult phase, one she saw as a failure at the time. Urja shared with me in her interview how, as a starting professional, she felt it was daunting to try to have a positive impact. She didn't feel well-equipped with either skills or experience, nor sufficient clarity of how the journey would unfold.

During her re-alignment phase, Urja's father, founder of Setco Automotive, took on a project as part of the Corporate Social Responsibility of the company. This was long before Corporate Social Responsibility laws came into effect in India. His motivation was one of giving back to the community in Panchmahal, Gujarat, from which their family originally hailed in India. Knowing that Urja held dear their shared values of service and had always wanted to support communities, he invited her to join the project. The aim of the project was to eradicate malnutrition in young children. The initial scope of the project had been to build early childhood community centers, called anganwadis, for young children and for new mothers to access care and support services.

Urja took on the project in 2010. At that time, there was only one person in a part-time support role to support 150

The Relief of Self-Leadership

preschoolers in 1 community. The annual operating budget was about $10,000 since most of the funds had gone towards capital expenses of the building and infrastructure. Once the building had been built, the initial services delivered, and the toys and learning materials distributed, Urja, who was a new mother herself at the time, reflected upon the real depth of impact of the initiative. She realized that there was a need for solid evidence of impact. Using her scientific background, Urja applied the training from her days as a researcher in biochemistry and policy to this new domain. She sought expertise from public health experts and sought to identify and distill the data to define the deeper "why" and "how" of the project. Urja looked at the real goal they were trying to meet, and through deep insight and community involvement, looked closely at what might be potential barriers to success. She was supported by a brave and inspiring woman named Salma who has been instrumental in shaping these initiatives on the ground. They found that child malnutrition was tied to many variables such as child development, maternal health, and awareness levels. At one point, she and her team rolled out a training program for young mothers only to realize that no one was willing to attend for months. Discouraged, they went back to look at the why. Urja and her team honed in on mindsets and cultural narratives that prevented the young mothers from joining the program. Her team adjusted and began to address the mindset and cultural narratives to build trust with the communities they were aiming to serve.

Today, nine years after they began this journey, Setco Foundation serves on average 9,000 to 11,000 people annually in 22 communities, including 2,300 preschoolers. Urja's biggest celebration from this project is the profound shifts she has seen in the community. She describes how girls are now staying in school, graduating from grades 10 and 12. Some go on to obtain Masters' degrees and MBAs. The young women who once were frail new mothers are now entrepreneurs, running family businesses, and independent women respected in their communities. Some have enrolled their husbands as business partners; others run their businesses independently. Some young women have taken on martial arts and gone on to represent their state at the national level. Urja shares the story of a young woman who learned the family pottery and clay trade and expanded the family business. As an acknowledgment of her contribution to the family, her father handed the family wheel called "chakdo" to her instead of her brothers. This indicates a profound cultural shift in the role of women. As of the 2019 fiscal year, Urja's team was composed of 40 members and managing an annual budget of around US $200.000, a 20X increase since 2010.

As a leader, Urja shares that there were times in her journey when she questioned her direction, her ability to bring about change, and her leadership. What kept her going was anchoring in her "why," giving herself space for different contemplative practices, and recognizing her mentors and allies on the journey. She learned to let go of perception and allow her team to grow and discover their own learning opportunities from "failures." She learned to mentor, and coach her team. She once had the humbling realization that she was not indispensable yet was responsible for the outcomes.

What I find deeply touching about Urja is the humility and authenticity with which she undertakes her endeavors.

The Relief of Self-Leadership

While she may not have known what her purpose was at the beginning, she gave herself permission to explore, step into the path unfolding before her, bring her knowledge and skills to an area she was not specialized in, and instead of imposing solutions, she and her team humbly met the communities they were attempting to serve and learned from them how they could best support them. She holds that the complete trust in her vision and leadership by her father and the board of the Setco Group, along with incredible technical and knowledge partners such as SNEHA & UMMEED, were hugely instrumental in her success as a fantastic operating team that is always learning and growing. In this way, Urja combines the power and relief of Self-leadership in partnership with impact allies.

Hero 2

Nhial Deng is an inspiring 23-year-old young man. For a decade, he lived in Kakuma, Kenya. Before that, he lived in Ethiopia where his father had settled after fleeing Sudan's brutal civil war nearly half a century ago. In 2010, his village was stormed by armed militias, Nhial had to separate from his father who was expected to stay behind and fight. At the age of 11, he walked for 2 weeks with women and kids from the village to reach Kenya's Kakuma Refugee Camp. At the camp, Nhial was able to enroll in school until he graduated from high school in 2018. Despite all the hardships he endured, Nhial had a dream of being a journalist and remained determined to finish his studies. In his senior year in high school, he was enrolled in the program Empowering Children as Peacebuilders (ECAP) by World Vision Kenya. Through the program, he heard stories similar to his from displaced youth, and he realized he had been blessed to overcome the trauma of his experiences while others had not been as fortunate. The realization ignited his desire to make a difference in his community. He founded the Refugee Youth Peace Ambassadors and began conversations with other youth, creating supportive spaces for them to heal through storytelling, meditation practices, mindfulness, mentorship sessions, game and sports activities, peacebuilding workshops, and music. In just one year, the Refugee Youth Peace Ambassadors reached out to more than 1000 young people in the Kakuma refugee camp and Kalobeyei integrated settlements.

After completing high school, Nhial didn't have a straightforward path to university just like many young refugees across the globe. But he did not allow this to stop him from pursuing his dreams. He took advantage of a number of online programs available in the refugee camp to learn about things he is passionate about. He enrolled in the Amala's Peacebuilding Course, Jesuit Worldwide Learning's Learning Facilitator Course, and finally FilmAid Kenya's Media Training Program, which he graduated from in June 2021. He also continues to get involved in community-based projects and play a key role in the establishment of projects such as StepUp.one to access employment opportunities and Kakuma Innovation Labs School.[59]

Answering my question about the changes he has witnessed, Nhial shares the story of Solomon from South-Sudan who established a youth group for peace in South Sudan after participating in one of their peace programs in the camp. Nhial shared with me about the moments in his journey when he felt discouraged and wanted to give up. When he turned 18 years old, he was suddenly removed from the

The Relief of Self-Leadership

United Nations High Commission for Refugees (UNHCR), the UN Refugee Agency child protection program that had been providing him with books, clothes, and other essentials. He wanted to give up, but the memory of his promise to his father that he would pursue his journalistic dream gave him the strength and courage he needed to find alternatives. This is when he stepped up and turned to stories of personalities who inspire him in history. He named leaders like Nelson Mandela, Mahatma Gandhi, John Lewis, and Martin Luther King. His meditation and contemplative practices supported him in continuing his journey, healing himself, and finding renewed hope and purpose through his initiatives. He finds his work deeply meaningful. In a very natural and humble manner, he declared that "service is the rent we pay for being on the planet" as said by Muhammad Ali.

In May 2021, Nhial was awarded a four-year scholarship to study at Huron University College in Canada where he is currently pursuing a bachelor's degree in Global Studies and Communications. In late December 2021, during the winter break, he traveled back to Kakuma to set up SheLeads Kakuma, a six-month long empowerment, advocacy, mentorship, and college-preparatory program for young girls and women in Kakuma refugee camp.

When he looks back at his journey, he is most proud of impacting more than 1000 young people in the camp with his activities and amplifying the voices of young refugees on several occasions. Nhial's story commands admiration and awe for the resilience of the human spirit, and the impact possible when one is aligned with their purpose.

Shero 3

A few years ago, a client reached out to me to support her in her leadership journey. We had interacted together through a speaking engagement and a common friend. She was feeling exhausted from trying to bring about change through her work and wasn't sure how to continue moving forward.

As the co-representative of the single parent association in the capital city of her country, the cultural context was particularly relevant to address. Single mothers are socioeconomically vulnerable in her culture, lack social support, and face a high level of discrimination due to stigma around single parenting. Knowing the culture and having been a single parent myself in the past, I was able to relate to the realities of single parents in a culture similar to mine.

We worked on shifting the areas where the cultural narrative of single parents was disempowering as well as with the principles of the Empowerment triangle to address where it was impacting her leadership and relationships. When we addressed her self-care, she gave herself permission to care for her well-being by delegating work. As her well-being started to improve and the emotional impact of her experiences processed, she started to feel stronger, navigated challenges with clarity, and transformed conflicts that had been impacting her ability to achieve her vision. She was able to manage her time differently and finished her M.A. As she clarified her vision, she and her team began to look at culturally sensitive and appropriate ways to bring change.

A few months after our work, I received a message that her organization had been able to impact policy in her country, getting single parents new benefits to which they were not previously entitled. A couple of years later, her work was recognized at the national level. As a result of her pursuing her vision and using the inquiry and processing practices, she was able to transform her blocks and bring change to a marginalized segment of the population.

> *PRINCIPLE #8*
> *Collective transformation begins with Self-leadership.*

Practice: Becoming the Leader You Have Been Waiting For

One of the most inspiring people I came across is my dear friend and author, Martin Rutte. Martin is the Founder of Project Heaven on Earth. For more than three decades, Martin has been inspiring everyday (s)heroes to take small actions towards becoming the change they wish to see in the world. I love that his work makes the idea of a completely upgraded life experience accessible to all of us and invites each person into action. When I met Martin, he asked me the three questions of Project Heaven on Earth:[60]

1–Recall a time when you experienced Heaven on Earth. What was happening?

2–Imagine you have a magic wand and, with it, you can create Heaven on Earth. What is Heaven on Earth for you?

3—What simple, easy, concrete step(s) will you take in the next 24 hours to make Heaven on Earth real?

I invite you to reflect on these questions and take one step towards creating your Heaven on Earth this week.

The Relief of Self-leadership

The healing journey has been long. I have been through cycles and seasons of healing. Each cycle gets easier. Yet, there were, and still are, moments of discouragement. Especially when an old pattern re-emerges and demands the next level of healing work.

When I began training as a coach, I felt the axis of my life shift... as if my life moved from one of closed doors to a life of possibilities. Coaching gave me the skills and mindset needed to stop running away from problems. Instead, I learned to pause, inquire about what was happening to me, and find solutions. With these tools, I started a new career. I turned around the Korea experience, and I began trusting myself more. I began to see that while I did not have the answers, I had a way of finding them. Time after time, I came out of sessions in awe. Seeing the quality of my life improve, my relationships enhanced. I began to listen to my dreams more than my fears. I had a way to excavate my buried courage out from under skepticism and discouragement. I let go of the fear of not having answers. Anxiety began to reduce. And trust began to increase. Day by day, I experienced the difference between powerlessness and self-responsibility. I learned to lead my own life. I learned that, in reality, nothing happened to me. Every difficult situation had invited me to higher possibilities.

The Relief of Self-Leadership

It took me time to step into Self-leadership and agency around not only my life but also the impact I would like to have to create a better world. I believe a better world is possible, and we are at a unique moment of opportunity, and sadly, of the old patterns of destruction re-emerging. Each one of us stepping into Self-leadership makes a difference toward creating a world where everyone can live in dignity and peace. What relief would Self-leadership bring to your life?

Poetry is one tool that connects us to the right-brain skills of visioning because it opens up the heart and mind to new possibilities. As you reflect on your relationship and vision for your leadership, I offer you this beautiful poem by poet and philosopher, John O'Donohue. In my own journey to Self-leadership, I found this poem to be a profound anchor.

A Poem for Leaders

May you have the grace and wisdom
To act kindly, learning
To distinguish between what is
Personal and what is not
May you be hospitable to criticism
May you never put yourself at the center of things
May you act not from arrogance but out of service
May you work on yourself
Building up and refining the ways of your mind
May you learn to cultivate the art of presence
In order to engage with those who meet you
When someone fails or disappoints you
May the graciousness with which you engage
Be their stairway to renewal and refinement
May you treasure the gifts of the mind
Through reading and creative thinking
So that you continue to be a servant of the frontier
Where the new will draw its enrichment from the old
And you never become a functionary
May you know the wisdom of deep listening
The healing of wholesome words
The encouragement of the appreciative gaze
The decorum of held dignity
The springtime of the bleak question
May you have a mind that loves frontiers
So that you can evoke the bright fields
That lie beyond the view of the regular eye
May you have good friends
To mirror your blind spots
May leadership be for you
A true adventure of growth

John O'Donohue

"Peace is the result of retraining your mind to process life as it is, rather than as you think it should be."
~Wayne W. Dyer~

CHAPTER 9

The Realization of Peace and Purpose

"I don't want to have that conversation. You deal with it." I hung up the phone and stared out the window.

What's really happening here? My husband usually listens to me, and it feels like he is not hearing me. I'm sure he is exhausted and overwhelmed with all he is going through right now. Yet the stakes are high for us. We have to find a new home. And there is so much uncertainty. How will I deal with this? I don't even have time to figure it out with so many moving pieces. But I know, something is amiss. I can feel it in my gut.

I was exhausted. Two months earlier, my daughter and I had returned to Canada in an emergency evacuation amidst the uncertainty of the Covid-19 pandemic. Our government had called for all Canadians abroad to return home; and in the span of thirty hours, our lives were packed in a few suitcases, and we were on a flight home.

My husband and I decided he would stay behind. We had left Canada because foreign service was his way of serving our country, and he couldn't bear the thought of leaving when Canadians were in the most dire time abroad. I knew this was important to him. As we decided together, we cried, worked through all the possible scenarios, and went to tell our daughter that only she and I would be flying home. We had no answers as to when we would be together again, where my daughter and I would go, or whether we would return to our posting or resume our lives in Canada.

My daughter still had to finish the school year remotely, and I had put my work on hold until I reached Toronto. But at this moment, while we were looking for a new home, we were operating on a stressful schedule. I worked with my Asia clients early in the mornings and late evenings and Europe clients in the afternoon while supporting my daughter with virtual school. I barely had time to eat in between the house chores, the work schedule, and my work which had been very demanding.

This is a critical point. The hard work of the previous years has come together, and I am not about to stop, I thought as I put the phone down and began tidying my desk while I processed.

To complicate my already busy and difficult schedule, my husband and I had to coordinate our schedules across Asian and North-American time zones to do virtual house visits. We were exhausted, each of us on one side of the world, living in the midst of collective panic as the pandemic unfolded. The stress was draining our resilience. We had been through difficult moments together, but this was a whole new ball game. He was working twenty-hour days, in complete isolation and had not seen a single soul for more than two months. He wasn't sure he would have access to the local network of food supply as a foreigner. So of course, he had a lot on his mind.

The Realization of Peace and Purpose

I understand that what he is going through is awful, but he needs to be accountable with me for the difficult decision ahead. The real estate market was extremely volatile and unpredictable. Even the real estate agents had no idea how to predict or give advice. There were very few homes for sale and, of the few available, prices were skyrocketing. We saw homes go for $100,000 more than the price asked.

Ugh, I've got to turn this around. As much as I felt tired, I had to be more resilient. He was not able to hear me, much less find a solution. And I wasn't able to articulate it much better. So I did the only thing I know to unlock my stuckness: I stopped and looked within.

I am angry at him. I am angry at the real estate agent for not listening. And my anger is covered up by confusion. I knew I'd gotten to the real issue when I felt the emotion.

I cried it out, journaled about it, spoke with close friends, and got support.

When looking inward, I found my anger was because I felt helpless and confused. My intuition kept telling me the homes we were seeing were outside of our price range; and it seemed that no matter how much I asked the real estate agent, all he lined up were homes outside our budget. "If you don't get more aggressive about buying, you will not find a home." But bidding above what we could afford was not a solution for me. It felt irresponsible, like setting ourselves up for future problems. I was being triggered by the fear-based approach to this purchase, even though I could feel he was really trying to help. I only had my intuition to go on, and it was telling me to work with someone else. I could not make sense of why.

It won't change the market prices, I argued within myself. *What if I am wrong? What if the agent gets upset? My husband has put the entire responsibility on me, and I will be blamed if this goes sideways.* But I had spent time and energy deepening my recognition and trust in my intuition; and I was no longer willing to ignore it because I knew the cost would be high.

Finally, I gathered my courage and called the agent.

I let him know that I saw the strength in his style, but for me, it was creating stress rather than motivation. That energy was not working for me. He understood, and we closed the transaction; and he referred me to another agent. I smiled when, after our first conversation with the new agent, my husband called me to say he finally understood what I meant. The contrast had enabled him to recognize the difference of feeling heard and supported.

Finally, four months after being back, and several moves later, we found the right home for our family. Not only within our price range, but it was one of the most beautiful homes we had visited and perfect for our family. My daughter had finished her school year, and I was launching my first group course online. I had been managing the launch with a virtual team, running my business, offering free community calls to support collective resilience through the stressful times, house hunting, and spending up to four hours a day on the phone with my husband to support him in the aftermath of the traumatic experience he had just gone through.

On September 5th, 2020, I woke up and facilitated the first live session of my program. My husband and mom began to move suitcases into the new house. I ended the session, my heart filled with gratitude and peace.

Using all of the tools I had acquired across my journey, I had done it. I had managed to create peace outside of me by first creating peace within me, even during one of the most challenging years most of us have faced individually and collectively.

> **DISEMPOWERING BELIEF #9**
> Peace is outside of us.

Peace, Purpose, and Positive Impact

Anxiety, fear, and grief are dominant emotions in today's world; and silent despair is an epidemic that is likely to grow after we move through the collective moment of reckoning brought on by the Covid-19 pandemic.

We are moving through times where our very safety in being together is shaken, a time during which we have become afraid of sharing the same space or breathing with each other. I suspect that much like a trauma response, once the acute phase passes, an emotional crisis will hit. The sense of powerlessness and loss of control will leave many grappling with this phase of their lives. Relationships will break, jobs will be lost, workplaces will need to adjust, and systems will need to change. We will ask ourselves the hard questions and adjust our direction. All that is not on solid ground in our current lives will be shaken and the cracks we held together, at any cost, will be impossible to ignore. The truth of the senseless striving we have been entrained to will need to be faced, and a new world will emerge.

In fact, this has already begun; and it may be exactly what drew you to this book in the first place.

Like butterflies, we will enter the metamorphosis phase, a phase where the darkness is strongest just before the light. As scary as this journey might seem, there are roadmaps and guideposts for it. There are many of us who have been navigating these waters of transformation, sitting in its fire, sharpening our tools, and learning to emerge lighter and brighter from the densest darkness. An understanding of the cyclical nature of life and the metaphorical cycles of death and rebirth will help us navigate the emerging transformations. We have the choice to experience this phase as a debilitating trauma, or transform the trauma into light. If you find yourself in doubt and fear, consider that this journey may "not be the darkness of the tomb, but rather the darkness of the womb."[61]

Despite the constant cycle of fear on the news, this last century has been the least bloody time in our history. We have strengthened our ability to meet our needs through the agricultural and industrial revolutions. Our physiological needs are taken care of at earlier stages than in previous generations, giving us access to the felt sense of safety required to self-actualize. Yet we have gone on to cater to ignorance and greed, rather than embrace our interconnectedness with nature and other beings. We have lost our way, indulging in ego desires rather than meeting

The Realization of Peace and Purpose

our soul needs. Our psychological needs are therefore asking to be seen and met. But we remain stuck because we view this invitation to transformation through the outdated framework of the linear life model.

When we see life from a higher perspective, with an interplay of shadow and light, we recognize illness, social unrest, and anxiety can be metaphorical deaths. We acknowledge they can be the soul's way of letting us know we are in misalignment. A way that the accumulated negative experiences of life are asking for our attention to peel away the layers of heaviness and darkness, so we can find our way to light and peace.

The practices shared in this book will help you to start turning toward and meet the heaviness... instead of running away from it. This simple practice of turning toward the discomfort will make all the difference in your life and determine whether or not you reach your goals and live your purpose. For some, these practices will be sufficient. For others, like me, questions will lurk in the background. Why didn't things work out? What am I missing? Where did I go "wrong"?

> When "why" is the central question you are looking to answer, you will likely only find peace through purpose.

I have found on my journey that the answers began to emerge as I aligned my life and work with my core values and purpose. Bringing coherence and harmony between who we are and what we hold as most important in life, and serving it with our skills and strengths will lead us to inner peace, resilience, harmony, and positive impact. One of the first things we must do as leaders of our own lives is shape our routines, relationships, and environments around what works for us. Many of us are unable to remain confined in the structures of the corporate world, or our chosen careers. The dysfunction of toxic environments does not allow us to apply our gifts to solving the real issues. Instead, it costs us our well-being and becomes draining. I began to shift from self-blame around this when I began to explore characteristics of highly-sensitive people, shaping my work around who I am, and helping others do the same. In my program, Do What You Love and Love What You Do, I support individuals wanting to open up to their purpose in taking their first big step to alignment. One of the elements we address is their winning environmental formula. This is one pathway to purpose.

The Realization of Peace and Purpose

Work as an Expression of Well-being, Joy, and Positive Impact[62]

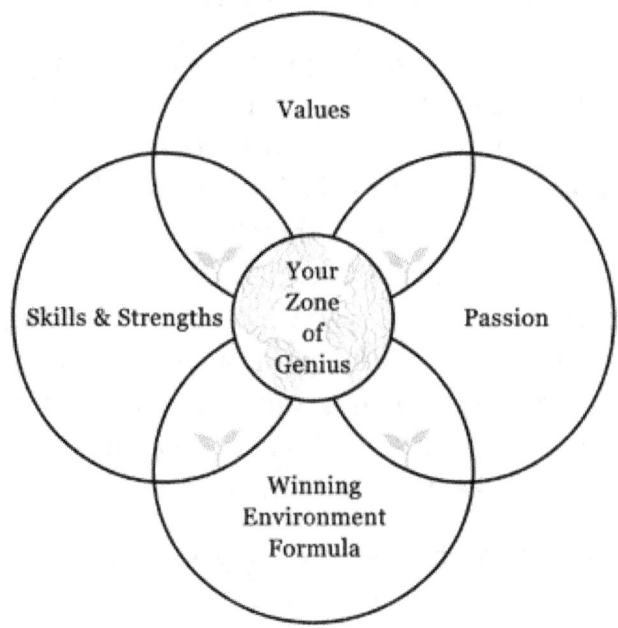

Many Paths to Purpose

One of the biggest misconceptions about aligning with our purpose is that it happens with ease and flow. Though I know this does happen for some, it has not been my experience; and I believe it's because of the wrestling match that happens between our ego and soul. It is indeed true for some people, as was the case for True Purpose® Coach, Beth Scanzani, who, within two years of committing to her purpose, was living in her dream location, doing meaningful work, and feeling much more aligned.

My own process was a bit longer, and more complicated. I will share the lessons I learned from exploring purpose through both Eastern and Western lenses.

Our ego is in charge of keeping us safe from perceived threats. This means that every time we get triggered, our ego sends us an alarm signal. It becomes very important to recognize when our ego is triggering fear because it is a perceived, rather than a real, threat. This allows us to break through the fears we will encounter and still move forward on our purpose path. The ego will use seductive objections to keep us in our current life path, such as falling sick right after deciding to invest in our transformation, losing our job or financial safety net, or a sudden problem that requires our attention and makes us believe we need to step back.

This is in fact the biggest difficulty we encounter before committing to our purpose. On one hand, we think we are ready. We declare our desire to live a more meaningful life, and align with our purpose, and suddenly it feels like our plans have gone for a toss. In reality, this is only a symptom of deeply held beliefs creating resistance. We could make sense of the experience by deciding we failed in finding our purpose, or we were not meant to live our purpose.

In my own life, I went through a few years where I gave up on my purpose because I misinterpreted things going "wrong" as meaning I failed at finding it. This is what happened when I had come back from Egypt with the feeling that I had a second chance at life and that I wanted to use what I had experienced to ensure others don't have to go through the same thing. Yet, I was vastly unequipped to deal with the depth of what I had experienced; and I had missed the

The Realization of Peace and Purpose

mark in that I wanted to fight the old systems rather than put my energy and time into creating a different life and impact. Later, as coach and coach trainer, I had a first-row seat to witness hundreds of people unlocking the hidden resistance from the ego and moving forward in their purpose path despite it. While my ego self was deeply pained by the traumas, I can also now recognize that, at a soul level, these experiences were leading me to a different path.

I recognize that when these "tragic" events show up, they are a part of our hero's/heroine's journeys. This is, in fact, the best time to practice mindfulness, use our inner witness, and name and transform the painful emotions and disempowering beliefs triggered by the experience. There is nothing more rewarding in life than becoming powerful in the face of our fears and suffering, and creating alignment with our soul's purpose.

The ego will try to tell us that we can think our way into our purpose. If we have depth, groundedness, and flexibility, it may work. However, if we have a more rigid belief system than we realize, or if we are attached to the linear model as I was, our journey will be blocked unless we let go of the resistance. The difficulty is that we may not recognize the places where our mindset is too rigid to allow our purpose to unfold with ease. Resistance and lack of ease will be our indicators that deeper healing needs to take place to shift our mindset, and therefore experience of life.

For example, we commit to aligning our work with our values and passion, and yet we find ourselves at the edge, unable to take the leap of faith and leave. Or we take the leap and live in so much fear and doubt that we barely move forward. I did a similar thing before I found the True Purpose® process.

When my dream of being a lawyer and making a difference in the way I had imagined fell apart, I thought I had failed, that I was never going to make sense of or succeed on this journey called life. It turns out that what was flawed was my understanding of how purpose unfolds.

Our purpose tests us and educates us about the ways of the soul. It gives us repeated opportunities for alignment until we choose to explore what is not working and change the unconscious disempowering belief system holding us back. If we are reliving a painful pattern in relationships, professional life, or other areas, we are being offered opportunities to break through each time. Painful as this process might be, it is liberating to stop spinning in circles and begin the breakthrough journey. And the more we do, the more we will access inner peace.

A Guide to Aligning with Your Purpose

The first stage of your purpose alignment is a form of training ground where you face your shadows. After a triggering event such as a job loss, death, an illness, or simply a deep internal shift, you will begin to sense things are different. You will find your need for silence deepening. You may find yourself less drawn to distractions, such as entertainment and social media. Even your conversations might start to feel shallow and uninviting. You will likely suddenly long for authenticity in every area of your life. You may be asking or praying for

The Realization of Peace and Purpose

answers and, suddenly, you come across someone who shares a message that sounds like exactly what you needed to know. Or you see a billboard, hear a song, or are gifted a book, or anything else that seems to be speaking exactly to the question you had. Small, seemingly meaningless synchronicities begin to unfold.

You can easily dismiss them, and yet something in you makes you wonder if they are more than random coincidences. This is the start of connecting with intuitive guidance. Most clients I worked with seem to receive this intuitive guidance primarily through their learning styles. Dreams or images for the visual learners, songs or audio content for the auditory, gut feelings or body sensations for the kinesthetic learners. At this stage, clients are often wondering which career move to make. They are usually torn between the logical answer, and the intuition they have that taking a different path is what they need. I see this especially with clients from professional backgrounds. They are the visionaries who see what is not working, yet they constantly blame themselves for not fitting in. Often drawn to many disciplines beyond their professional background, their gift of seeing feels like a curse because it has not yet been acknowledged. They remain stuck, afraid of letting go, until they begin to trust their vision and intuition. If you are in this stage and do not tend to it, you can remain there for years. At this stage, getting support from someone who has an understanding of how purpose unfolds can make all the difference.

The second stage of purpose is adjustment. After acting on your intuitive guidance, notice to what extent the new choice brings you to a space of ease, flow, and impact. When your actions do not have sufficient flow and impact, you need to continue your introspective practices to align yourself further with your purpose. This dance between your inner world and the outer world is what cultivates your trust in your purpose and your path.

Purpose has seasons and cycles. You may feel you are regressing at the beginning of every cycle. You are, in fact, progressing; but the non-linear nature of how purpose unfolds will invite your inner critic, based on your left-brain thinking, and make you think you are not moving forward. It will even make you wonder if you should go back to "safer ground"—like a normal job.

You will recognize a purpose cycle coming to an end by no longer feeling drawn to the people you met or the type of work you were doing at the beginning of the cycle. It may be through conflict or a simple lack of resonance. This is no one's failure. It simply is an indication the cycle has served its purpose, that you learned what you needed to from the cycle and the people who walked it with you.

> *The process of letting go might be uncomfortable, but the more you learn to recognize your purpose's seasons and cycles, the more peace and gratitude you find with endings.*

You will also find that what started with ease and flow starts to feel much more effortful, and you will feel your attention and drive either going down or towards other endeavors. When your drive goes down, it does not mean you are depressed or lazy as your inner critic might want you to believe. The

The Realization of Peace and Purpose

body needs to integrate what you learned, and sometimes recover from the intensity of situations. Make more space for your contemplative practices and give yourself time for self-care, rejuvenation, integration, and reconnection to your inspiration. The next cycle will open up. The more you resist this process, the longer it will take. Truly, the best thing you can do in this phase is allow your body, mind, and soul to rest and nurture yourself. If you do have a history of depression, or you are concerned, do seek medical advice immediately.

For me personally, going through the True Purpose® Process as a client answered the "why" questions, and gave me much relief from the anxiety of not knowing. It was so impactful for me that I later got trained as a True Purpose® Coach.

What's the link between purpose and peace?

> *The paradigm of purpose naturally leads you to a more peaceful life, where you feel connected to yourself, others, and nature.*

Your personal life, your relationships, and your work become more satisfying, providing you effortless joy and simplicity. Your desire to contribute to living in a better world grows, and your ability to apply your skills and strengths to your areas of impact increases. You move to a paradigm of Self-leadership and responsibility where you become the change you wish to see in the world. Your courage to step into bolder visions increases, and if your willingness meets your desire, you can truly expand your impact.

The greatest inspiration for me has been Dr. Scilla Elworthy. She is an example of living these skills and making a large-scale impact. She has taken on bold visions such as bringing nuclear arms makers into conversations around disarmament and peace. She is the author of the *Business Plan for Peace,* in which she demystifies the goal of making peace on earth a reality, with concrete, tangible, and proven solutions, and a financial plan to execute this endeavor. I had the opportunity to interview Dr. Elworthy for our Wellness Webinar Series from June 2020 on the topic of Linking Inner Work to Leadership Outcomes.[63] Her insights are inspiring, and she has recently written a book called *The Mighty Heart* where she shares the qualities we need to cultivate in order to step into the leadership required to tackle big challenges.

Research shows that individuals who are connected to their purpose reap the benefits in every area of life. Even their leadership is improved by up to 63%, and their fulfillment and health increase by more than 30%. Companies with a connection to their purpose have been shown to see their profit margins increase significantly and be more inclusive.[64] This shows the power of purpose in action, and the importance of living our lives, not from the highly-limited and fragmented lens, but rather from the interconnected nature of the soul.

With all this *evidence* available, I wonder what more we need to *catalyze* a radical shift in our ways of being?

The Realization of Peace and Purpose

Breaking The Cycle

At the start of our session, my client shared that she had been selected to do a Ted Talk; and while a part of her was very happy about the opportunity, she was unable to move forward or put together her content. She was confused about her resistance.

We engaged with her inner critic and found it was loudly shouting at her that she was stupid and not good enough because she wasn't excited. She was also weighed down by feelings of not being good enough to share her message. Why her, and not someone else? Was what she had learned enough? Would the audience resonate? Would she sound like a fool? All these were running in her mind below the surface level of the stuckness.

And then there were concerns about the story itself. Spreading a message that is related to one's purpose can bring up a strong feeling of vulnerability. This is because our purpose is usually tied to some of the most difficult experiences we have had. That is also why healing is an integral part of living our purpose and why the pain gets triggered at the beginning of each cycle. With every cycle, the pain reduces and our ability to recognize it, move past it, and clear it gets stronger.

There comes a point when the pain is simply a memory, and we reap the rewards of having done our healing work: working from ease, synchronicity, and joy while contributing to society in ways that are most meaningful to us.

In this specific session, we did the clearing work required; and in a matter of hours, the client was able to write her content, clarify her message, and get past the imposter syndrome that was lurking in the background. She was supported by a TEDx Coach to hone her presentation skills, clarify her message, and feel clarity and ease in sharing her message. She went on to present her talk and even teach others how to step into the journey of preparing for a TEDx talk. As she continues to grow strong in her connection to purpose, she continues to touch more lives and earn more recognition.

While stepping into purpose might be a challenging endeavor, it is a journey that brings us fulfillment, meaning, wellness, and coherence. I have traveled the world, lived in beautiful places, met amazing people, and yet I found purpose to be the most beautiful and peaceful destination.

> **PRINCIPLE #9**
> Outer peace can only be attained through inner peace.

Practice: Dear Future Self Connection

Give yourself the gift of a calm space where you can self-connect and allow yourself to daydream and tap into the future.

Take some quiet time to reflect on a future version of yourself that would make you excited to wake up every day. A version of you that has re-written the disempowering stories of your past, and turned into an empowered and joyful version of

The Realization of Peace and Purpose

you, growing in flow and in the abundance that goes far beyond material objects.

What does this future self look like?

Where is this future self physically? What does the space around them look like?

What feelings are they experiencing?

Give yourself time to deepen this image, and stay with it as it unfolds. After a few minutes, approach your future self and ask: What does my life look like from here?

Allow it to describe what its days look like, what it finds joy in doing, and with whom it enjoys spending time. Invite whatever else it wants to share with you.

If you do not like to use imagery, you can do this exercise as a self-guided reflection. Imagine that you are waking up with a sense of satisfaction and enthusiasm for the day ahead, and answer the same questions.

How valuable would it be for you to live this life? Are you willing to take the brave steps to get there? Whatever your answer is, write a letter to your future self and share with them why you are accepting the call to step into a higher version of your life, or not.

Keep this letter somewhere safe and mark your calendar to re-read it in exactly one year. You may be surprised by the unfolding.

My Realization of Peace

As I closed the last suitcase, put my computer in my bag, and set off for our new home, I took a moment for a gratitude prayer.

We were tested, and we passed.

Everything I had been releasing to make room for a newer and more resilient and empowered version of myself had been tested. My health, my balance, the safety nets I had created. All of that had been stripped away in thirty hours, and our family was nearly torn apart from the stress of it all. My husband was bruised psychologically, my daughter was tired of the moves, and we were all exhausted from the uncertainty.

We came into our new home to find a beautiful welcome card and a few gifts! We had made it, together, stronger than ever, despite strong shaking in our foundation the previous months.

This is the power of inner work. Stopping and tending to the energy, emotions, and beliefs behind stuckness brings me to inner peace; and from this state of deep presence and surrender, new solutions and outcomes unlock. Once again, I had experienced the relief of Self-leadership to weather life's harsh storms and turn conflict into peace.

My purpose was my anchor in the troubled waters of this entire experience.

CONCLUSION

From Inner Work to Leadership Outcomes

"Assalam Alikoum." My heart fluttered as I spoke those words, which mean "Peace be upon you," at the opening of a peace-building project with a group of dedicated individuals from Yemen. I was moved to tears seeing the beaming faces on my screen. Everyone present felt the energy. Being a part of a team of global mentors bringing our support to a peace initiative for Yemen was deeply meaningful.[65]

This moment felt like a milestone for me.

It was the opening of a new chapter in the story of one young woman, on a quest for identity and belonging, in a complex world. Bringing all I had learned together, using my skills, and following my soul's calling, I was now stepping into a new cycle of my purpose: Bringing a message and tools for peace, hope, resilience, empowerment, and oneness.

As I wrapped up the call, I once again sat with polarities in my heart. On one hand, feeling deeply fulfilled to be bringing much-needed skills and attention to a team working for peace in Yemen, a country forgotten by the world and facing a war eclipsed in the priorities of those who hold the strings of power globally.

Simultaneously, I felt a deep sadness. I had spent the weekend reading, brainstorming, and speaking with the peacebuilding community about what we could do to support those fleeing Ukraine.

There is no denying our attention to world events suffers the same biases that drive our interactions.

The words of Mahatma Gandhi felt more real than ever: "Our ability to reach unity in diversity will be the beauty and the test of our civilization."

As I write these words, the world is still grappling with many wars. The war in the Ukraine, however, hits closest for the Western world. It shakes our belief that Europe has risen above war; and if Europe is not, is anywhere above war? So here we are, caught in the cycle of violence again. One toxic leader was sufficient to create suffering and fear on a large scale *again,* awakening us to the reality that we can never take peace for granted.

Simultaneously, we are witnessing a new type of leadership in Volodymyr Zelenskyy—a leader who acts from authenticity, courage, and compassion. This is the new type of leadership needed to make peace a reality on Earth. A leadership that stands firmly in the face of tyranny—a leadership from presence, with the ability to interrupt the patterns of the past and create a different future.

And while in the past, this type of leadership was understood to be a way of being, it is now accessible by design. This is precisely the leadership my work enables. It is the type of leader I have become after decades of trial and error, after much deep work.

Ever since I began studying coaching, I noticed a couple of constants in our world.

From Inner Work to Leadership Outcomes

> *Our soul longs for peace,*
> *and our shadow thrives in conflict.*

As we are mostly driven by the unconscious dynamics of our collective shadow, the only way to a peaceful world is a sustainable time and energy investment in clearing our shadows and building internal and external infrastructures for peace. I knew this to be true even years before I began peace-building work.

And suddenly, in 2021, it all came together as I worked with Dr. Scilla Elworthy. After many years of working to influence policy, she came to the conclusion that peace is only possible if we make it a priority in our day-to-day lives.

Throughout this book, I have endeavored to disavow the false beliefs many of us have been operating under. Much of what we believe has been enforced through culture, social customs, and accepted practices; but not everything we have been taught aligns with our values and ideals. When there is dissonance between that which we genuinely hold to be true and that which intuitively feels inconsistent, we experience a crisis within ourselves. That crisis manifests itself in ways that impacts our physical, mental, social, and emotional well-being, though it will be different from individual to individual.

Leaders tend to look at the world in its disarray and feel restlessness, a calling, or even anger; but many will not allow themselves to sit in and dissect that emotion due to fear or insecurity. If that's you, it is important to know that this fear is keeping you from knowing your best self. As individuals, we allow false beliefs to hold us back from operating from a place of alignment where joy, purpose, and growth trisect. When we accept that which is put in front of us without questioning why our intuition and emotions rail against these practices, we are choosing to live apart from our authentic selves.

To know that authentic self requires an internal journey, where we examine our beliefs, experiences, and emotions to identify the underlying values and needs. As we do so, we find those moments of inner peace where our whole mind is applied to our passions and the impact we endeavor to make. We become our own (s)hero, saving ourselves before seeking to impact others or the world.

What if you made the choice to start treating your own self with the respect you demand of others? What if you started by listening to your own thoughts and emotions without judgment, but acceptance? Your best companions on this journey are honesty, courage, and compassion. They open the door to the inner peace you will derive from the practices in this book as the first steps to a more truthful, purposeful life.

The knowledge of self carries within it a more universal knowledge of the world and the humanity in all of us. This understanding will help us to behave with empathy, compassion, and kindness. And with that will come the peace we seek both within ourselves and within the world. The most important asset you will need for this journey is your willingness and ability to unlearn and relearn more productive ways of being. As the eloquent words of Alvin

Toffler offer: "The illiterate of the 21st century will not be those who cannot read and write, but those who cannot learn, unlearn, and relearn."

I believe that if we are willing to embrace our collective shadow, we can create a more peaceful world, yet it hinges on a critical mass of us being an agent of peace and facing our own individual shadow material.

Our future is not yet written. We shape it with each decision we make, with each action we take and, most importantly, with each action we *do not* take. If we are serious about creating a peaceful world, our words, thoughts, and actions will need to reflect it as a priority.

I believe we are collectively at a critical time in history, shaping the future of the human race. We cannot delegate this important work to future generations because their very survival is at stake. If ever there was a time to rise up, and take action, it is now. And at all levels. From kitchen tables to policy advisory meetings, from boardrooms around the world to United Nation talks, we need to make Self-leadership the norm rather than the exception.

Will we seize this moment collectively? Will you seize it individually? Bring it to your boardrooms? To your community?

Years from now, as you are taking your last breaths, what story do you want to tell about how you unfolded peace from the inside-out? What role will you have played?

A Special Invitation

Through this book, you've learned the 9 principles and done some wonderful work to deepen your awareness; and you may be feeling like you need more.

Maybe you need some support on your healing journey, or a structured dive into the topics, held in a container by someone who has been on the same path.

Perhaps some accountability would be helpful.

Maybe you wish you had peers—a global community— that understands your journey and speaks the same language.

Maybe you would like to bring this work to your organization, or to decision-makers.

This could be the beginning of our journey together!

Come join us at **www.ConsciousTogetherness.com** and take a look at the ever-unfolding ways we are working to create a world where everyone can live in dignity and peace, and how we can support you as you unfold peace for yourself and those around you.

About Kawtar

As a conscious leadership consultant, coach, facilitator, mentor, and speaker, Kawtar El Alaoui, LL.B, PCC, partners with conscious leaders and organizations to create cultures of well-being, belonging, and peace.

After years of searching and experimenting with methods of driving change, Kawtar found that the changes we truly wish for in our hearts, and for our world, must be unfolded from within. Having supported leaders from all walks of life, and diverse cultural backgrounds, to find peace with the past and cultivate more empowering dynamics for themselves and their communities, Kawtar uncovered a new paradigm of empowering, uniting, and effective leadership. In The Conscious Togetherness Leadership Framework®, she weaves tools for deep inner healing and meaningful service to guide leaders in creating a more equitable, peaceful, and prosperous world. Crafted to bring humanity back to business and systems, this model offers principles and tangible tools for self-awareness, conscious communication, and collaboration, conflict transformation, social equity, trauma-informed relating, and personal and organizational purpose.

As a consultant, Kawtar bridges whole-brain leadership, soul purpose, and effective strategy. Her legal background and mediation training, combined with her leadership profile, give her access to a systemic view that holds the interests of diverse stakeholders with equal care. Her gift for creating spaces of deep listening to self, and the collective, allows individuals and cultures to turn wounds into wisdom, unleash the courage to create systemic change, and establish new life-enhancing paradigms in the spaces in which we lead.

Kawtar was voted 2020 Global Woman of the Year in the category of education by the Global Institute for Evolving Women. She was featured in Women's News Korea and by Brainz magazine for International Women's Day 2022 as 1 of 7 female entrepreneurs changing the world and awarded a CREA Global Award for her contribution as a Leadership Coach and Facilitator. Kawtar is the Founder & CEO of Conscious Togetherness, Inc; Faculty and Mentor with International Coaching Federation accredited coaching school, Leadership That Works India; a Facilitator with Business Plan for Peace in the UK; and a Leadership Advisor with She Did It! Elle a osé! in Canada.

Kawtar enjoys bonding over deep conversations, diverse cultural traditions and foods, and collaborating on innovative and effective solutions to social problems. When she's not speaking, coaching, or changing the world, she's home cooking delicious Moroccan food for family and friends or watching her favorite shows on Netflix.

Endnotes

1. nikita.sheth@upskilledsolutions.com

2. Cégep is a publicly funded, 2-year pre-University school system, exclusive to the province of Québec in Canada.

3. Peter Lacy, Katherine LaVelle, and Alberto Zamora, Whole-Brain Leadership: The New Rules of Engagement for the C-suite, June 2019. "Striking Balance with Whole-Brain Leadership: The New Rules of Engagement for the C-Suite." Accenture, June 5, 2019. https://www.accenture.com/gb-en/insights/strategy/whole-brain-leadership-for-c-suites.

4. Cherry, Kendra. "The 6 Types of Basic Emotions and Their Effect on Human Behavior." Verywell Mind, January 13, 2020. https://www.verywellmind.com/an-overview-of-the-types-of-emotions-4163976.

5. Gabor Mate, *When the Body Says No: Understanding the Stress-Disease Connection,* Wiley, 2011.

6. David Servan-Schreiber, *The Instinct to Heal: Curing Depression, Anxiety and Stress Without Drugs and Without Talk Therapy,* Rodale Books, 2004.

7. Perry, B. D., Pollard, R. A., Blakley, T. L., Baker, W. L., & Vigilante, D. (1995). Childhood trauma, the neurobiology of adaptation, and "use-dependent" development of the brain: How "states" become "traits." *Infant Mental Health Journal, 16*(4), 271–291. https://doi.org/10.1002/1097-0355(199524)16:4<271::AID-IMHJ2280160404>3.0.CO;2-B

8. Creswell, J David et al. "Brief mindfulness meditation training alters psychological and neuroendocrine responses to social evaluative stress." Psychoneuroendocrinology vol. 44 (2014): 1-12. doi:10.1016/j.psyneuen.2014.02.007

   Katharina Star, PhD. "How to Use Relaxation Techniques for Help With Anxiety Disorders." Verywell Mind, September 17, 2020. https://www.verywellmind.com/popular-relaxation-techniques-2584192

Hölzel, Britta K et al. "Mindfulness practice leads to increases in regional brain gray matter density." Psychiatry research vol. 191,1 (2011): 36-43. doi:10.1016/j.pscychresns.2010.08.006

9. Mindfulness Center at University of California in Los Angeles: https://www.uclahealth.org/marc/

10. Mitzi Baker, Undoing the Harm of Childhood Trauma and Adversity, UCSF Weill Institute for Neurosciences, October 2016.

11. Brown, Brené. "The Power of Vulnerability." TED, June 2010. https://www.ted.com/talks/brene_brown_the_power_of_vulnerability?language=en.

12. Adapted from The Center for Non-Violent Communication https://www.cnvc.org/training/resource/feelings-inventory

13. Ibid.

14. Ibid.

15. Ibid.

16. Adapted and expanded version of Karpman's Drama Triangle.

17. Brown, Brené, and Oprah Winfrey. "The Stories We Tell Ourselves," November 25, 2015. https://www.youtube.com/watch?v=WyK537UA_E8.

18. Mcleod, Saul. "Maslow's Hierarchy of Needs." Simply Psychology. Simply Psychology, March 20, 2020. https://www.simplypsychology. org/maslow.html.

19. Brickman, P et al. "Lottery winners and accident victims: is happiness relative?." Journal of personality and social psychology vol. 36,8 (1978): 917-27. Mcleod, Saul. "Maslow's Hierarchy of Needs." Simply Psychology. Simply Psychology, March 20, 2020. https://www.simplypsychology.org/maslow.html.

20. Ibid.

21. Adapted from The Center for Non-Violent Communication . https://www.cnvc.org/training/resource/needs-inventory

22. Ibid.

23. https://www.conscioustogetherness.com/do-what-you-love

Endnotes

24. Porath, Christine. "Why Being Respectful to Your Coworkers Is Good for Business." TED, January 2018. https://www.ted.com/talks/christine_porath_why_being_respectful_to_your_coworkers_is_good_for_business/footnotes.

25. Ouimet, Maeghan. "The Real Productivity Killer: Jerks." Inc. Magazine, 2012. https://www.inc.com/maeghan-ouimet/real-cost-bad-bosses.html

26. Seppala, Emma, and Kim Cameron. "Proof That Positive Work Cultures Are More Productive." Harvard Business Review, May 8, 2017. https://hbr.org/2015/12/proof-that-positive-work-cultures-are-more-productive.

27. Elworthy, Scilla. *The Business Plan for Peace: Building a World without War*. London, UK: Peace Direct, 2018.

28. Author Dave Eggers in conversation with President Barack Obama. Obama Foundation, November 20, 2018. https://www.youtube.com/watch?v=N7ZHD0NhScY

29. For more from my interview with Dr. Scilla Elworthy, and how she links the tools of inner work to leadership outcomes, you can purchase the Webinar Series Find Your Path to Wellness: Go Deeper, Rise Stronger. One third of the purchase price is donated to The Business Plan For Peace: https://www.conscioustogetherness.com/find-your-path-to-wellness/

30. Goh, J., Pfeffer, J., & Zenios, S. A. (2015). The relationship between workplace stressors and mortality and health costs in the United States. *Management Science*, 62(2), 608-628.

31. "Workplace Stress Continues to Mount." Korn Ferry, November 14, 2018. https://www.kornferry.com/insights/articles/workplace-stress-motivation.

32. Eleesha Lockett, Emotional Signs of Too Much Stress, Healthline, August 2018. https://www.healthline.com/health/emotional-symptoms-of-stress

33. David Servan-Schreiber, *The Instinct to Heal: Curing Depression, Anxiety and Stress Without Drugs and Without Talk Therapy*, Rodale Books, 2004.

34. Dr. Brian Goldman. "The Power of Kindness: Why Empathy Is Es-

35. Ruairi Robertson, PhD, "The Gut-Brain Connection: How it Works and the Role of Nutrition", Healthline, modified August 2020, https://www.healthline.com/nutrition/gut-brain-connection

36. "Learn More about Dr. Marie." Bioheal Ottawa, May 4, 2019. https://biohealottawa.com/learn-more-about-dr-marie/.

37. L Groff, "Intercultural communication, interreligious dialogue, and peace," Futures, Volume 34, Issue 8, 2002, Pages 701-716

38. Hari, Johann. "Everything You Think You Know about Addiction Is Wrong." TED, 2015. https://www.ted.com/talks/johann_hari_everything_you_think_you_know_about_addiction_is_wrong?language=en.

39. Taylor, Jill Bolte. "My Stroke of Insight." TED, February 2008. https://www.ted.com/talks/jill_bolte_taylor_my_stroke_of_insight?language=en.

40. To find your personalized path to wellness, you can purchase the Wellness Webinar Series, Find Your Path to Wellness: Go Deeper, Rise Stronger. One-third of the purchase price is donated to The Business Plan For Peace: https://www.conscioustogetherness.com/find-your-path-to-wellness/

41. Channel 5 News. (March 26, 2018). The Campaign to end male suicide. [Video file]. Retrieved from https://www.facebook.com/567036616654154/videos/1825120120845791

42. OECD, Investing in Women and Girls: The Breakthrough Strategy for Achieving All the MDGs, June, 2010, Accessed December 24, 2020. https://www.oecd.org/dac/gender-development/investinginwomenandgirls.htm.

43. David E. Bloom, Michael Kuhn, and Klaus Prettner, "Invest in Women and Prosper", FINANCE & DEVELOPMENT, September 2017, Vol. 54, No. 3

44. Juliana Menasce Horowitz, Ruth Igielnik and Kim Parker. "How Americans View Women Leaders in Politics and Business." Pew Research Center's Social & Demographic Trends Project, August

7, 2020. https://www.pewsocialtrends.org/2018/09/20/women-and-leadership-2018/.

45. Tomas Chamorro-Premuzic, Cindy Gallop, "7 Leadership Lessons Men Can Learn from Women", Harvard Business Review, April 2020. https://hbr.org/2020/04/7-leadership-lessons-men-can-learn-from-women.

46. Noland, Marcus & Moran, Tyler & Kotschwar, Barbara. (2016). Is Gender Diversity Profitable? Evidence from a Global Survey. SSRN Electronic Journal. 10.2139/ssrn.2729348.

47. Richard Wellins and Evan Sinar, *The Hard Science Behind Soft Skills*, Development Dimensions International, May 2016.

48. Marie O'Reilly, Andrea Ó Súilleabháin, and Thania Paffenholz, "Reimagining Peacemaking: Women's Roles in Peace Processes," New York: International Peace Institute, June 2015.

49. Karaarslan, Birsu. "From Being Victims of Gynocide to Becoming Sheros", 2020.

50. PBSfrontline. "A Class Divided (Full Film) | FRONTLINE." YouTube. YouTube, January 18, 2019. https://youtu.be/1mcCLm_LwpE

51. Rollin McCraty and Doc Childre, "Coherence: Bridging Personal, Social and Global Health", Alternative Therapies, Jul/Aug 2010, VOL. 16, NO. 4.

52. Lacy, Peter, Alberto Zamora, and Katherine LaVelle. Rep. *Striking Balance with Whole Brain Leadership: New Rules of Engagement for the C-Suite*. Accenture Strategy, June 5, 2019. https://www.accenture.com/us-en/insights/strategy/whole-brain-leadership-for-c-suites

53. van Bezooijen, Nienke. "Listening to Restore Peace." YouTube. YouTube, December 4, 2020. https://www.youtube.com/watch?v=gPNc2UHWRJY

54. McKinsey & Company, Diversity wins, how inclusion matters May 2020. https://www.mckinsey.com/featured-insights/diversity-and-inclusion/diversity-wins-how-inclusion-matters

55. Adichie, Chimamanda Ngozi. "The Danger of a Single Story | Chimamanda Ngozi Adichie." YouTube. YouTube, October 7, 2009. https://www.youtube.com/watch?v=D9Ihs241zeg.

56. https://www.ltwindia.com/

57. McAuliffe, Christopher D. "The Coaching Show: Talking ACTO and Intuition on Apple Podcasts." Apple Podcasts, October 8, 2020. https://podcasts.apple.com/us/podcast/talking-acto-and-intuition/id1448785589?i=1000494043772.

58. Mezzofiore, Gianluca. "This Danish Ad Will Challenge You to Step Outside Your Defining Box." Mashable. Mashable, January 31, 2017. https://mashable.com/video/danish-ad-all-that-we-share-box

59. StepUp.One, Re-Skilling Refugees and Connecting them to Opportunity, World Economic Forum, February 2019. https://stepup.one/

60. Martin Rutte, Project Heaven in Earth: Three Simple Questions That Will Help You Change The World…Easily, Livelihood, 2018, pp.13-17.

61. Valarie Kaur, Civil Rights Activist Delivers Passionate Speech for America, January 2017, https://valariekaur.com/2017/01/watch-night-speech-breathe-push/

62. https://www.conscioustogetherness.com/do-what-you-love

63. Finding Your Path to Wellness: Go Deeper, Rise Stronger is a low-cost webinar series about pathways to wellness. ⅓ of the proceeds from your purchase will be donated to Peace Direct, and contribute to building peace: https://www.conscioustogetherness.com/find-your-path-to-wellness/

64. "The Science of Purpose." Accessed May 6, 2022. http://scienceofpurpose.org/.

65. SAM Organization for Rights and Development, 2023, https://namati.org/network/organization/sam-organization-for-rights-and-development

www.ingramcontent.com/pod-product-compliance
Lightning Source LLC
Chambersburg PA
CBHW071904290426
44110CB00013B/1269